A word from the author

My first memory of pastoral visiting takes me back to when I was five. My Sunday School teacher arrived at our house to see why I hadn't been to Sunday School for weeks! Even now, I remember how guilty I felt. I remember getting a row from my mother because I continued playing with my dolls instead of speaking to our visitor. If I learned anything from that experience, it was to make sure that any pastoral visits I made later in life as a Sunday School teacher, youth leader or elder did not feel like a visit from the church attendance officer!

For twenty years now, I have had the privilege of working with pastoral visitors and elders in the Church of Scotland and in other denominations. I have been encouraged, challenged in my faith and humbled by the stories they have told. Some of these stories appear in the book but names and minor details have been changed in the interests of confidentiality.

In my role as pastoral visitor, I am indebted to all those who have welcomed me into their homes or hospital wards and shared their journey with me. They have helped my faith to grow and my skills to increase. I often think they have given more than they have received!

It is my hope and prayer that this book will encourage all who are involved in pastoral caring in the local congregation and community. Many challenges face the church in an increasingly secular society. How we care and how we are seen to care are crucial parts of sharing the reality of our faith.

Perhaps our situation is not so different from that of the early church, whose members made a significant impact on their surroundings by the quality of their care for one another. (Acts 2: 43-47)

Practical Caring

Introduction:

In response to many questions and enquiries, we hope to bring you, the potential church visitor, some of the answers necessary to enable you to do your job effectively. Sheilah Steven, the Board of Parish Education's Adviser on Eldership, has written a timely, sensitive and instructive book which will be of use for many years to come.

What is pastoral care?
What part does visiting play?
What qualities are necessary for the practice of pastoral care?
What resources are available to church visitors?
How can visitors meet the needs of those visited?

These are just some of the questions addressed here. Practical issues such as organising a visit, sensitivity, self-care and awareness will also be considered in the appropriate chapters, together with reflective exercises to stimulate thought or discussion in a group. This short guide cannot hope to cover the vast spectrum of human need, but we do hope that something of Christ's love as shown to the world through his body, the church, will impact on you and therefore on the world around you and the people you contact. Pastoral care is arguably the most important function of the body of Christ, 'By this everyone will know that you are my disciples, if you have love for one another' (John 13: 35).

Contents

What is pastoral care?

Christ has no body on earth but yours, no hands but yours, no feet but yours.
Yours are the eyes through which you must look out with Christ's compassion on the world.
Yours are the feet with which he is to go about doing good.
Yours are the hands with which he blesses now.

St Therese of Avila

These words of St Therese of Avila echo the words of Jesus at the last supper when, after washing the disciples' feet, he said to them, "Now, I give you a new commandment; love one another. As I have loved you, so you must love one another. If you have love for one another, then everyone will know that you are my disciples." (John 13: 34 & 35).

Christians through the ages have taken Jesus' words seriously and have been inspired to care for others in imaginative ways, appropriate to their age and cultural context. From the hospitality offered by monks, to education for children in every parish, to hospitals in remote parts of the world, to meeting the needs of the poor, Christian history shows many examples of caring in Jesus' name.

In the Church of Scotland, as early as 1581, Andrew Melville describes part of the elder's role as visiting the poor, the sick and prisoners, and encouraging them in their faith. Times may change, but the need for a caring Christian community expressing the love of Jesus remains as important as ever.

How do we nurture the children and young people in our midst?
How do we effectively care for single people both old and young?
How do we support families?
How do we care for those going through times of difficulty and crisis?
How do we encourage those in leadership positions in church and community?
How do we care for those who no longer wish attend our church?

These are some of the pastoral care questions that congregations need to explore. You might like to investigate those questions further, perhaps in a small group in your church.

As a part of pastoral caring, local congregations usually have a visiting programme designed to encourage and sustain their members and others in the community. Recognising the gifting of all God's people, some congregations have already appointed pastoral visitors to share in the ministry of care alongside elders. These visitors are people who are not necessarily ordained elders in the Church of Scotland.

However it is organised, pastoral care is a response to Jesus' command to 'love one another.' It is a challenge to all Christians whoever and wherever they are. It is a responsibility of the local congregation to care in appropriate ways for those connected with its life. It motivates congregations to reach out to those who suffer injustice, pain and deprivation in the local community and beyond.

Reflection Points - to be considered on your own or with others

Reflection 1

List all the practical ways that your congregation cares for its members and the community in general.

Reflection 2

Pastoral care has been described as, 'Reflecting the unconditional love of God to others.' Pastoral Care Revisited Frank Wright

How true has this been in your own experience of visiting and being visited?

Reflection 3

Story - an example of pastoral care:

Jack's wife died. They had no church connection but the local minister, through careful listening, conducted a meaningful funeral service. Jack recognised his wife in the music, the prayers and the readings. As he left the crematorium, he said to the minister, "I might come to your church sometime."

Jack started to attend church regularly. He received a warm welcome at the Sunday morning service and invitations to church events. He was surprised and pleased to receive occasional visits from the minister, and regular visits from the elder and the pastoral visitor.

Jack never joined the church and as his health declined was unable to attend church any longer. The visits, however, continued even when he was hospitalised. He proudly showed off to visitors and staff the church flowers he had received.

What does this story say to you about pastoral care in the local church?

Reflection 4

Jesus is recorded as saying:

God's spirit is on me
He has chosen me to proclaim the Message of good news to the poor
sent me to announce pardon to prisoners and
recovery of sight to the blind,
to set the burdened and battered free,
to announce, "This is God's year to act!"

(Luke 4: 18-19 The Message)

To what extent could this be considered as the church's manifesto for pastoral care?
What other biblical passages might you consider as such a manifesto?

Reflection 5

A Prayer for Love

God of all goodness and grace,
you are worthy of a greater love
than we can either give or understand.
Fill our hearts with such love for you,
that nothing may seem too hard for us to do or to suffer
in obedience to your will.
And grant that, loving you,
we may daily become more like you,
and finally obtain the crown of life
which you have promised
to those who love you;
through Jesus Christ our Lord
Amen

Book of Common Order of the Church of Scotland

Further thought:

If you are reading this now, you might well be considering pastoral care and you will know what your congregation considers to be appropriate training.

The Church of Scotland, through its Elder Trainer Network, provides an opportunity to develop pastoral care skills. There are also many 'care in the community' type courses on offer from local authorities to NVQ level or above.

It is always possible to discuss practical issues and develop a pastoral care infrastructure with other congregations seeking to do the same things.

Being a Church Visitor

To be welcomed into someone's home is a privilege. It is not a right. Sometimes it has to be earned because people have had a bad experience of church visitors in the past.

Consider for a few minutes the people you like visiting your home. The chances are that they are open and friendly. They know when it's convenient to come and they don't overstay their welcome! You share interesting news and celebrate together. They listen to what you have to say. You think of them as friends and know that they would help out if you were having a difficult time. They are people with whom you can relax and be yourself.

This model of friendship seems a good one for church visitors who seek to reflect the love of Jesus. The visitors might be elders visiting homes in a district on a regular basis. They might be pastoral visitors who assist elders in this work. Some will visit those who are housebound, or have been bereaved, those in hospital or residential homes, young families, or young people and children. What practical steps can improve our visiting in these differing situations?

As a first step it is important to remember that we are going in the name of the church, in Christ's name. We are not alone! David Scott, an Anglican vicar, has written a book on prayer and pastoral visiting, called *Moments of Prayer*. In it he says, 'A visit that is born out of prayer can never really be just a social visit. You lay it before God for his blessing, help and inspiration.'

If this is a first visit, introduce yourself as coming from the church. The previous visitor may accompany you or have briefed you on the visits you are to make. The church might have sent a letter of introduction for you. Hopefully the person you are visiting will not be taken by surprise!

When is the best time to visit? To a large extent this depends upon whom you are visiting. Visitors sometimes find that making a prior phone call to fix a convenient time works well. The elderly might enjoy a visit on a long winter evening but would not open the door to an unexpected visitor. The busy family would not appreciate the visitor arriving just as the toddler is going to bed! Arriving in the middle of a favourite TV programme can be a problem in some homes, unless you sit and watch with them until it is finished.

How long to stay? For some people, in certain circumstances, twenty minutes will be long enough. For others, an hour will seem too short. Be guided by the person you are visiting and by how long you can reasonably give.

Keeping a notebook to record important dates, events and names will allow the visitor to respond to events in people's lives. Sending a birthday card or phoning to ask how the exam went can build up real friendship with those whom you visit. The notebook can also serve as a guide to prayer.

Involving people in the life of the church can be an important part of the visit. A church magazine, the order of service, the church flowers or a prayer card might be welcome. Taking a tape of the church service and listening to it with a housebound person can be very worthwhile. Seeking people's opinions on issues affecting the church and asking them to pray can make them feel a valued part of the church community.

An example

One church prepared an attractive bookmark with a Bible verse and some suggested items for prayer. Visitors gave these to the housebound who consequently felt more involved in the life of the congregation.

Sometimes people will share things that are confidential with a church visitor. Only share what you have been told when you have the person's permission. Gossips are not trusted church visitors! If your church has a prayer network or book for recording prayer requests always ask if the person would like to be included and ensure that you have the correct wording of the request.

When criticism comes, a church visitor needs to be loyal to the minister, elders and church members. You are all part of the one team. Do encourage the person to address their concern to the appropriate person, or promise to investigate any cause of complaint yourself.

Remember you are part of a team and do not have to bear all the responsibility for the person you are visiting. Sometimes on a visit you might become concerned about the physical, mental, emotional or spiritual needs of the person visited. Do discuss the situation with the minister or pastoral co-ordinator. If such a situation arises, it might be appropriate to inform the nearest relative, check with your team first. Help may also be available from the local GP, the community nurse, the duty social worker/welfare rights officer, Citizen's Advice Bureau or support groups such as Alzheimer Scotland or ChildLine. National help lines are listed in the BT phone book.

Lastly, it's worth saying something about self-care at this point. In an ever-increasingly time-pressured society, think carefully about how much time you can give to pastoral visiting. Everyone is busy and there are so many things to do. Discipline in time spent away from home will benefit the pastoral visitor so that he or she does not feel burdened by the task or the situations of the people s/he might meet. Visiting is not something for which you need to be a qualified social worker. As we've said before, refer to your church, minister or pastoral care co-ordinator any situation where you are uncomfortable, and be very clear about the amount of time you are able to give.

We hope you'll find the following exercises helpful in observing your attitudes to relationships and in setting boundaries for yourself and others:

Reflection 1

Alastair Campbell in his book, *Paid to Care* says, 'Pastoral care has one fundamental aim: to help people to know love both as something to be received and as something to give.' How true have you found this to be in your own experience of visiting and being visited?

Reflection 2

Building up good relationships is crucial to good pastoral care. John Powell (in his book *Why Am I Afraid to Tell You who I Am?*) states that the quality of a relationship depends on the quality of communication. He identifies five levels of communication:

Building Relationships

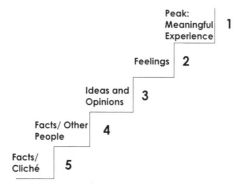

Level Five communication can be about the weather, the garden, holidays. It is a 'nodding' acquaintance. If asked 'How are you?' the level five answer would be 'Fine!' It can open the way for deeper communication.

Level Four communication is about facts and other people. The facts shared can be about the church, the news, TV programme, the other person's job or family.

Level Three communication is about sharing your own and the other person's opinions and ideas. This is more risky because it involves revealing more of yourself. Hostility, criticism or rejection might result in sharing at this level.

Level Two communication is about sharing feelings with each other. This demands a degree of honesty and vulnerability which is not easy for many people. 'Why am I afraid to tell you who I am? Because you might not like who I am and that is all I have to offer!' (Socrates)

Level One is perfect communication. It involves complete openness and honesty, is usually fleeting and often without words. You just know you have communicated at the highest level possible.

Consider the five levels of communication in the diagram. Can you identify one person from your own network of relationships (at work, in your family or with people you regularly meet or visit) for each level of communication?
Are there people with whom you would like to move up a level? If so how would you go about it? Do you think they would welcome deepening your relationship?

Spend some time in prayer about this.

Reflection 3

In the parable of the sheep and the goats, Jesus commends the 'sheep' by saying:

> I was hungry and you fed me,
> I was thirsty and you gave me a drink
> I was homeless and you gave me a room
> I was shivering and you gave me clothes
> I was sick and you stopped to visit,
> I was in prison and you came to me.
>
> (Matthew 25: 31-46 *The Message*)

To what extent does this challenge how we build up relationships, and with whom, as we seek to care in Jesus name?

Listening

Christians have forgotten that the ministry of listening has been committed to them by him who is himself the great listener and whose work they should share.

> 'We should listen with the ears of God that we may speak the words of God'.
>
> Dietrich Bonhoeffer

When Job, in the Old Testament, was experiencing extreme suffering he was visited by well-meaning friends who proceeded to share with him their theories as to why all these things were happening to him. Job responded, "Listen to what I am saying; that is all the comfort I ask from you." (Job 21: 2 *GNB*)

A key skill in caring for others is listening. Giving the person your undivided attention, focusing on them and putting your own anxieties to one side are very important. Many visitors find that a prayer for God's blessing prior to the visit - even as you approach the door - can help to focus on the person visited and their needs.

When people are experiencing difficult times they often find it valuable to have someone who will listen to them without necessarily offering them advice. The value of being alongside, of accompanying those going through difficult times, should not be underestimated.

A good listener is someone who respects other people and their experiences. In Matthew, the words of Jesus are a challenge to all pastoral visitors!

> "Why do you see the speck in your neighbour's eye but do not notice the log in your own eye?"
>
> (Matthew 7:3 *NRSV*).

A judgmental attitude towards the way others think, speak or act will hinder good listening. "How could anyone live with wallpaper like that?" is an unlikely question to be in a listening visitor's head!

Listening carefully to others, giving them our undivided attention, is a skill worth learning. Often when we think we are listening when we are in fact thinking up our reply or preparing to share our own experience. It has been suggested that we spend a third of our listening time doing just that! It is also important to hear what people are not saying. As an example - why might the elderly lady you visit never mention her daughter who stays in a neighbouring town?

The social scientist Dr Albert Mehrabian did some research into what cues people use to judge whether another person likes them or not. The other person's actual words contributed only 7% to the impression of being liked or disliked, while the tone of voice contributed 38% and the body language 55%. A church visitor who is aware of the facial expressions, tone of voice and general appearance of the person they are visiting will have a better under-standing of what that person's words really mean. Equally, it is perhaps important to remember that the church visitor's effectiveness may depend more on the manner of their visit than on what they say.

Eye contact is a particularly important component of body language. We tend to distrust people who do not look us straight in the eye. If we are talking to someone and their eyes are looking elsewhere, we doubt their interest and sincerity. Looking at your watch during a visit sends a negative signal! Letting your eyes be drawn to the television in the corner also suggests a lack of interest in the person you are visiting.

Learning to tolerate silence while a person struggles to articulate their thoughts can be useful to a pastoral visitor. It is so easy to finish someone's sentence for them or say "I know exactly how you feel" - when it is obvious to all concerned that you haven't even begun to understand. If a silence persists, summarising what the person has already said can help them to continue. It also reassures them that you have been listening!

Asking questions when you don't understand something that has been said can encourage the speaker. Sometimes answering your question can clarify their own thoughts. Remember that 'why' questions can sometimes make people feel defensive. Much better to use an open question such as 'How would you see that working out?' which encourages thoughtful reflection.

Listening to ourselves can help to improve our listening to others. It might be that you feel uncomfortable visiting a particular person. Ask yourself why that might be. Do they remind you of some terrifying teacher you once had? Does their bereavement make you feel uncomfortable because you have been unable to come to terms with bereavement in your own life? Does their negative attitude to life challenge your Christian faith? Reflecting on those kinds of questions before God, on your own, or with a group you trust can help you to develop as a pastoral visitor.

Listening to God was a crucial part of Jesus' ministry. He withdrew to be alone with God and to listen. In John 5 Jesus says, "I can do nothing on my own; As I hear I judge, and my judgment is just, because I seek not to do my own will but the will of him who sent me." (John 5: 30 *NRSV*). In busy lives it can be difficult to listen to God. Activity takes over. If, however, we are seeking to care for God's people as pastoral visitors, the challenge is for us to be aware of God's voice speaking to us. 'Where is God in this?' is a question we need to ask at the end of every visit. 'Where are you in this?' is a question we need to ask in our prayers.

Teach Me to Listen
Teach me to listen, lord,
   to those nearest me -
   my family, my friends, my co-workers.
   Help me to be aware that
   no matter what I hear,
   the message is,
   "Accept the person I am. Listen to me."

Teach me to listen, Lord,
to those far from me –
the whisper of the hopeless,
the plea of the forgotten,
the cry of the anguished.

Teach me to listen, Lord
to myself.
Help me to be less afraid
to trust the voice inside –
in the deepest part of me.

Teach me to listen, Lord
for your voice –
in busyness and in boredom,
in certainty and in doubt,
in noise and in silence.
Teach me Lord to listen.

Anonymous, from a collection by Brother John Veltri (SJ)

Reflection Points

Reflection 1

As you read the humorous poem below what do you think it might be saying to pastoral visitors about listening to older people?

I'm fine! How About You?
There is nothing whatever the matter with me,
I'm just as healthy as I can be
I have arthritis in both knees
When I walk, I talk with a wheeze,
My pulse is weak and my blood is thin,
But I'm awfully well for the shape I'm in.

My teeth will eventually have to come out
And my diet I hate to think about,
I'm overweight and I can't get thin,
My appetite's such that it's sure to win -
But I'm awfully well for the shape I'm in.

Old age is golden, I've heard it said
But sometimes I wonder as I go to bed,
My ears in a drawer, my teeth in a cup,
My eyes on the shelf until I get up,
When sleep dims my eyes I say to myself,
Is there anything else I should lay on the shelf?

I get up each morning and dust off my wits,
Pick up the paper and read the obits,
If my name is missing, I know I'm not dead,
So I eat a good breakfast and go back to bed.

The moral is this - as this tale we unfold:
That for you and me who are growing old,
It is better to say: "I'm fine" with a grin,
Than to let them know the shape we are in.

Anonymous

Reflection 2

Sandra, a young widow, welcomed her regular church visitor into her home. The television was on and the pair chatted about this and that, as they usually did. To the question, "How are things with you?" Sandra answered "Fine!" but the church visitor was aware that Sandra's hands were constantly on the move and she was barely aware of the TV, although it was quite loud and obtrusive to the conversation.

"And how are the children?" asked the visitor. Sandra almost said, "Fine!" but she hesitated and then started, "Things are not so good. I was summoned to the school today and..."

The story continued for thirty minutes with little being said by the visitor. Sandra gradually began to see the way ahead as the visitor asked what her options were for dealing with the situation. The visit ended with committing the whole situation to God.

What does this story say to you about listening and pastoral visiting?

Reflection 3

Psalm 139 from *the Message* (in three parts):
> God, investigate my life;
> Get all the facts firsthand.
> I'm an open book to you;
> Even from a distance you know what I am thinking.
> You know when I leave and when I get back;
> I'm never out of your sight.
> You know everything I am going to say
> Before I start the first sentence.
> I look behind me and you are there,
> Then up ahead and you're there too your reassuring presence, coming and going.
> This is too much, too wonderful -
> I can't take it all in.

Can you think of a time when you were especially aware of God's re-assuring presence?
Is there anything now that you need to be reassured about by God?

Continue reading Psalm 139:
> Is there any place I can go to avoid your Spirit?
> To be out of your sight?
> If I climb to the sky, you're there!
> If I go underground, you're there!
> If I flew on morning's wings
> to the far western horizon,
> you'd find me in a minute -

you're already there waiting!
Then I said to myself, "Oh he even sees me in the dark!
at night I'm immersed in the light!"
It's a fact: darkness isn't dark to you;
night and day, darkness and light, they're all the same to you.

What are your greatest fears?
In what way can God help you with these?

Reflection 4

Continuing Psalm 139…

Oh yes, you shaped me first inside, then out;
you formed me in my mother's womb.
I thank you, High God –you're breathtaking!
Body and soul, I'm marvellously made!
I worship in adoration –what a creation!
You know me inside out,
you know every bone in my body;
you know exactly how I was made, bit by bit,
how I was sculpted from nothing into something.
Like an open book you watched me grow from conception to birth;
all the stages of my life were spread out before you,
the days of my life all prepared
before I'd even lived one day.

(Psalm 139:1-16 *The Message*)

What does this say about God's love for you?
Spend some time in silence before God. Listen for anything he has to
say to you.

A Prayer for Faith in Difficult Times

Almighty and eternal God:

Our eyes cannot see you,

Our hands cannot touch you.

You are beyond the understanding of our minds.

Yet you have breathed your Spirit into our spirits.

We ask now for your blessing on

.......Insert name(s)....

as they face

......Insert the difficulty....

Give us faith to lay hold of things unseen,

To live as those who see the invisible God.

Through Jesus Christ our Lord

Amen

Book of Common Order

Further Reading:

The Wisdom to Listen, Michael Mitton, Grove Books, Cambridge, 1995

Listening to Others, Joyce Huggett, Hodder, London, 1988

Listening, Anne Long, Daybreak, London, 1990

Dibs in search of self, Virginia Axline, Pelican, London, 1971

Moments of Prayer, David Scott, SPCK, London, 1997

Pastoral Prayer

You can pray *with* them sometimes
but pray *for* them always.

Rev Geoffrey Studdert Kennedy
(Army Chaplain, 'Woodbine Willie')

Jesus, early in his ministry, went back to his home town. The people were impressed by his teaching but he could do no miracles there. It is recorded in Mark's Gospel that Jesus was greatly surprised because the people did not have faith. (Mark 6: 1-6 *GNB*)

Pastoral caring and visiting are part of the outworking of faith. They are ways of expressing God's love and care. Prayer is about acknowledging God's presence and seeking God's wisdom. Praying for the people whom we are visiting is an essential part of pastoral care.

How do pastoral visitors fit such prayer into busy lives?

Every Sunday, one visitor would go to church five minutes early so that he could pray for the people whom he visited. Another had a hectic life but, as she walked her dog, she would pray for the people whom she visited.

Keeping a notebook in which he recorded items for prayer for the people for whom he cared helped another visitor to pray meaningfully. He made sure that anything he put in his notebook he would not have been worried about showing to the people for whom he was praying.

Sometimes it can be difficult to know what to say in prayer. Picturing in our mind's eye Jesus blessing the people for whom we want to pray can help in situations like this. Visitors sometimes experience a feeling whilst in prayer that they should visit a particular person at a particular time.

An example

Ian had time for one more visit that evening. He had three more visits to complete. Where should he go? The names of one young couple came strongly into his mind. As he rang the bell, he was met by a distraught young husband whose wife had just been admitted to hospital as an emergency. He needed someone to talk to so that he could get things into perspective. Ian was just the right person at the right time. Ian's faith was strengthened that night!

Prayer is deep at the heart of Christianity. Jesus spent time in prayer as is recorded many times in the Gospels. His disciples were so impressed by his prayers that they asked him to teach them to pray and we now have the words of the Lord's Prayer. Jesus encouraged his disciples to pray. He said,

"Ask, and you will receive; seek, and you will find; knock and the door will be opened to you. For everyone who asks will receive, anyone who seeks will find, and the door will be opened to him who knocks. Would any of you who are fathers give your son a stone when he asks for bread?... How much more, then, will your Father in heaven give good gifts to those who ask him!"

(Matthew 7: 7-10 *GNB*)

Paul in his letter to the Thessalonians encouraged them to pray at all times and asked that they should also pray for him. (1 Thessalonians 5:17, 25)

St Therese of Avila reminds us that 'Prayer is a dialogue with the one we know loves us.'

John Wesley went so far as to say that 'God does nothing but in answer to prayer.'

Archbishop Temple said, 'When I pray coincidences happen. When I don't they don't.'

Prayer is not some sort of magic for pastoral carers. It is an acknowledgement that God is a vital part of the relationship we develop with others as we seek to care in Christ's name.

Most visitors feel comfortable with the practice of praying for the people they visit, but some can feel uneasy with the idea of praying aloud with another person.

For some, like Doris, the opportunity is thrust upon them

Doris, as a pastoral carer, went to visit an elderly lady in hospital. The lady talked about her operation and then asked Doris about her family and the church. Then she asked Doris to say a prayer for her. Doris was somewhat taken aback as she had never been asked to pray for anyone before. However, putting her trust in God, she said a simple prayer.

Others have more warning

Bob had been advised before he made his first visit that Jenny would ask him to say a prayer. He wrote out a prayer and took it with him and, much to his surprise, he enjoyed sharing the prayer with her. Each time he went, he wrote a different prayer. Eventually he didn't need to write them down!

Ellen felt that perhaps prayer should become more of a part of pastoral visiting. So she considered whom she might safely practise on! When asked, the selected couple were happy to have her say a prayer and suggested that they might pray for Ellen too! Prayer for each other became a regular part of that visit and deepened the whole relationship.

Annabel was sharing a difficult situation with her pastoral visitor. "Why don't we just have a time of silence while we share our thoughts with God?" suggested the visitor. They did and both felt refreshed by the experience.

Praying *with* people can benefit everyone concerned. 'Would you like me to say a prayer or would you rather say your own prayers?' might be an acceptable way of ensuring that prayer is not forced on a reluctant person. It's not a personal failure if people decline the invitation. However the young minister was surprised to hear the elderly lady saying, "By all means pray, if it makes you feel better!"

In his book, *You can make a Difference*, Tony Campolo writes,

> I have a twenty year old son, and I can't imagine him walking into our
> house and saying to me, "Oh, thou chairman of the sociology
> department at Eastern college, Oh thou who dost clothe me and feed
> me and provide me with every good and perfect gift; I beseech thee
> this day to lend me the car." That's not the way he talks to me. I'm his
> daddy. So like a good Italian boy, he walks into the house, throws his
> arms around me, kisses me and says, "Hi, Dad! Can I borrow the
> car?" You see we love each other. Jesus wants each of us to be
> intimate with him. That is why the apostle Paul tells us that we should
> not pray as people filled with fear, but we should talk to God as one
> who is closer than any could ever be. Actually the apostle Paul
> instructs us to address God as "Abba" which is the ancient Hebrew
> word for "daddy".

Tony Campolo

Pastoral prayer is at its best when it is short and spoken in simple everyday
language. Someone once described pastoral prayer as being like the four men
who brought their paralysed friend to Jesus. All they did was use their
imagination in getting their friend there and then left the rest to Jesus.
(Mark 2: 1-5)

The simple idea of laying a person and situation at Jesus' feet for his response is
at the heart of pastoral prayer. God is not going to be impressed by fine
language. It's the faith that counts. The belief that God will answer in his own
way and time is at the centre of pastoral prayer. In Jesus' words: "Come to me,
all you who are tired from carrying heavy loads, and I will give you rest."
(Matthew 11: 28 *GNB*)

A pattern for a simple pastoral prayer might be:

> Loving God, we have been talking about .... (situation)
> We bring this situation to you.
> Bless .... (name of person(s)) with your peace and strength.
> In Jesus name we ask this.
> Amen

It is important to use people's names in pastoral prayer and that is why a blank is left in the above prayer after the word 'bless'. Some people might never have heard their own name mentioned in a spoken prayer. Hearing their name spoken can make the prayer more real.

One visitor reported saying a prayer which asked, among other things, that the discomfort that a plaster-cast was causing the person should be eased. It was. The plaster split that evening! I don't know who was more surprised, the person or the visitor!

Other ways of sharing prayer on a pastoral visit can include:

A hand on the shoulder, or a hug (if appropriate – do be sensitive!) with the words, "God bless you".

Choosing a favourite verse of a hymn, psalm or poem and writing it on a card could be another way of sharing a prayer.

Saying, "I will pray for you", can be a comfort.

Some churches have prayer groups who will pray for those who wish it. Asking the person what they would like to have prayed for is a way of ensuring that confidentiality is respected.

Other churches have a book or box where requests are placed and appropriate prayer made. In this way everyone can be involved in the caring role.

Reflection Points to be considered on your own or with others:

Reflection I

Here are three versions of the Aaronic blessing:

i) May the Lord bless you and take care of you.
    May the Lord be kind and gracious to you.
    May the Lord look on you with favour and give you peace.

(Numbers 6: 24 -26 GNB)

ii) The Lord bless you, and keep you:
    The Lord make his face to shine upon you , and be gracious unto you:
    The Lord lift up his countenance upon you and give you peace.

(Church Hymnary 3: number 556)

iii) God bless you and keep you,
    God smile on you and gift you
    God look you full in the face
    And make you prosper.

(Numbers 6: 24-26 *The Message*)

Which version would you prefer to use and why?

What helps you in your prayers for others and what hinders your prayer?

Reflection 2

Read through the Gospel of Luke, preferably in a modern translation or paraphrase like *The Message* by Eugene Peterson, and see what you can discover about the prayer life of Jesus.

Reflection 3

Jesus was brought up on the Old Testament. Read the following and see what they say to you about prayer: Psalm 13, Psalm 23, Psalm 51, Psalm 73, Psalm 103, Psalm 121, Psalm 130, Psalm 139, Isaiah 55, Lamentations 3: 19-33

Reflection 4

In *The Peace of the Earth be With you* (song 121 in *Common Ground*), the following blessing was brought to Scotland by a Scottish Churches' World Exchange volunteer in Guatemala:

The peace of the earth be with you,
the peace of the heavens too;
the peace of the rivers be with you,
the peace of the oceans too.
Deep peace falling over you.
God's peace growing in you.

Common Ground

Are there any other worship songs you know which would make good prayers?

Reflection 5

Below are three prayers. How useful do you think they might be as pastoral prayers?

Gaelic Prayer

As the rain hides the stars,
as the autumn mist hides the hills,
as the clouds veil the blue of the sky,
so the dark happenings of my lot
hide the shining of your face from me.
Yet, if I may hold your hand in the darkness,
it is enough.
since I know that,
though I may stumble in my going,
You do not fall.

(Traditional Scottish, translated from the Gaelic by Alistair Maclean)

My Lord God, I have no idea where I am going,
I do not see the road ahead of me...
Nor do I really know myself, and the fact
that I think I am following your will
does not mean that I am actually doing so.
But I believe that the desire to please you,
does in fact please you

And I have I have that desire in all I am doing...
Therefore I will trust you always, though I may seem to be lost...
I will not fear, for you are always with me and you will never leave
me to face my troubles alone, O my dear God.

(Thomas Merton, adapted)

God, grant me
Serenity to accept the things I cannot change
Courage to change the things I can,
Wisdom to know the difference.

(Dr Reinhold Niebuhr, adapted)

Resources

Moments of Prayer, David Scott, SPCK, 1997 - a book on prayer and pastoral visiting
Video: *Caring for God's People*, unit on prayer Scottish Christian Press: Edinburgh, 1997

Prayer Anthologies:
Pray Now: Daily Devotions for the Year: Panel on Worship of the Church of Scotland, Saint Andrew Press Edinburgh, published annually

Various titles by Eddie Askew, prayers and meditations in modern down to earth language, published by the Leprosy Mission:
Disguises of Love
No Strange Land
Facing the Storm
Slower than Butterflies

Various titles by David Adam, published by SPCK:
Prayers in the Celtic tradition
The Edge of Glory
Tides and Seasons
Power Lines
The Open Gate

Prayers by Michel Quoist, published by Harper Collins

Visiting those who have been bereaved

Suffering is not a question that demands an answer. It is not a problem that requires a solution. It is a mystery that demands a presence. Suffering in another human being is a call to the rest of us to stand in community.

John Wyatt

Elders and church visitors often feel inadequate when they are visiting a bereaved person or family. David Winter, a retired parish minister and author has said, 'It may well be that the best possible qualifications for Christian service are that we don't feel worthy and we don't feel adequate for the task.' He cites the example of Moses who, in Exodus (chapters 3 and 4), tells God why he is not the right person to lead the children of Israel out of Egypt.

To someone who is visiting a bereaved person 'What will I say?' can be the thought which comes immediately to mind. This is particularly so if the death has been as a result of an accident, involves a child, or is sudden and unexpected. The longer you leave the first visit, generally the harder it becomes.

Where the visitor knows the bereaved well there can be a concern that they will be too emotionally involved. Paul's words in Romans 12:15, 'Be happy with those who are happy, weep with those who weep' can provide some reassurance.

Story

Jenny's daughter had been killed in a skiing accident. As soon as Bill, her church elder found out, he went to see her. Bill had a daughter the same age and the girls knew each other. When Jenny opened the door no words were spoken. Bill hugged her and they both cried.

That hug, the hand on the shoulder, the gentle hand-shake can express more than many words could convey. 'I was so sorry to hear about…' can often be the opening for the bereaved person to share something of their experience with a good listener.

It is the experience of most bereaved people that they need to share over and over again the story of their loss and to do so without interruption. They need to know that the visitor is listening and that they care.

Story

Elizabeth, the church elder, was making a normal quarterly visit. Carol invited her in and said, "Did you hear what happened to my father?" Elizabeth had not. Carol then began to tell Elizabeth about her father's sudden death on the golf course. Dave, Carol's husband went off to make everyone a cup of tea. For over twenty minutes the visitor sat listening. An occasional nod and 'Yes' were sufficient to encourage Carol to retell the story. Dave had heard the story many times before but he knew this was helping Carol to accept the reality of the death of her much-loved father. Elizabeth was a fresh pair of ears!

Sharing memories of the deceased can be healing. Avoidance of mentioning the deceased's name can cause pain to the bereaved.

Story

After sharing over forty years of marriage, Joe found Margaret's death hard to bear. People, even in the congregation, did not know what to say to him. They did not want to increase his sadness. The church visitor had known Joe and Margaret well. "I never did find out how you and Margaret met each other", he said, on his first visit after the family had gone home. Joe started to tell the story and before long the photograph album came out. "Margaret never could take a decent photograph!" Joe said, as they looked at a particularly out-of-focus shot of himself and the children, and he and his visitor both laughed.

Visitors need to be aware of children and young people's needs in a home where the adults are grieving. Has anyone spoken to the children and asked them if they would like to see the body and attend the funeral? Adults sometimes, in their grief, want to protect children by sending them away to relatives and friends and by not talking much about what has happened.

Children can feel excluded. They can feel that in some way they are to blame. Having someone who cares, who will honestly answer their questions and talk about the person who has died, can help children enormously. Sometimes drawing a picture of the person who has died can help a child to talk about what has happened and ask the questions they need to ask.

Some bereaved people might need practical help with transport, household management or finance. The sensitive church visitor can often access the church or community network for the assistance required. It is perhaps as well to remember that helping the bereaved to do things for themselves is better than completely taking over.

Although no two people will grieve in the same way, there are some features which are common to the experience of most people who are bereaved:

When we learn of the person's death, there is a shock which can range from a cold feeling in the pit of the stomach to fainting and hysteria. There is the numbness which serves to get us through those first days, the feeling of being on automatic pilot; the feeling that this is all a bad dream and we will soon wake up; the feeling that this is all happening to someone else.

There might be the physical symptoms of nausea, being unable to sleep, eating too much or too little, and feeling too hot or too cold. A lack of concentration can mean making a cup of tea is an effort; watching television is no help; and remembering what people have actually said becomes almost impossible.

Some people, who have not seen the body or have not been able to attend the funeral, may find that accepting that the death has actually happened can take a long time. Sometimes a child's room will be kept exactly the same, in the belief that perhaps one day they might come back. However, for most people, the funeral service begins the process of saying 'goodbye' and celebrating the life of the person now dead.

Bereaved people can feel the pain of the loss for months and years afterwards.

Feelings of guilt:

Why did I not realise he was so ill? If only I had tried harder, it might have been a better marriage. I caused the car accident, why did I survive? What did I do wrong as a parent that my son committed suicide? Did I drive her to the alcoholism that eventually killed her? Why did I never tell her that I loved her? Why did I not come to see my father more often?

Feelings of anxiety

How will I cope with finances? Can I let my other children out of sight or will something happen to them too? Am I experiencing the same symptoms that the deceased had? I don't feel safe in the house on my own.

Feelings of anger and bitterness:
Why did God allow this to happen? Why did she die and leave me with three children to bring up on my own? If the ambulance had arrived on time, my child would be alive now. It is so unfair.

Feelings of loneliness and emptiness:
What is the point of living now that my child is dead? What is the point of going on holiday on my own? I spent so much of my time caring for my mother, I don't know what to do with my time now.

When death comes after a long illness, a strong feeling of relief can be experienced. However the person who has been bereaved might also feel guilty because they do not feel as sad as they think they should.

Usually these feelings are strongest in the months following the death, but events such as Christmas, birthdays, the first anniversary of the death, can bring them back with renewed intensity. How people feel depends very much on the circumstances of the death, their quality of relationship with the deceased and their personality.

Sharing feelings is a form of healing. A visitor who can listen to the painful feelings without saying 'I know exactly how you feel' or 'time's a great healer' will be helping the person who has been bereaved to come to terms with their loss.

In Psalm 23: 4, the psalmist says, 'Even if I go through the deepest darkness, I will not be afraid, Lord, for you are with me.' Some bereaved people know the truth of these words in their heads, but it does not feel that way. To have a trusted visitor who will listen and provide help, where necessary, can help them to feel the presence and love of God in a real, tangible way.

It is generally accepted that two years is the average time for people to come to terms with bereavement. Two years to feel that life is worth living without the deceased, to be able to treasure memories without pain, to be prepared to start again, to develop new relationships and interests, to live without knowing why. For some it takes much longer.

Caring for the bereaved is about being there in the ups and downs; being aware of the difficulties of the first time of doing something again – like going to church; offering opportunities for the bereaved to use their skills and insights in helping others; assuring them of the prayers of the church family; leaving a prayer card; praying for them and perhaps with them.

Coming to terms with loss can be very similar to coming to terms with bereavement. A visitor caring for those who are separated or divorced; who have lost their job; who have been incapacitated in some way through illness or accident; who have lost their home or whose family have left home, will appreciate that those who are suffering also have to accept the reality of their loss, admit to their feelings and adjust to a different life. They, too, will struggle with strong feelings and wonder how they will cope. Having a listener who is not directly involved in the situation can provide an opportunity for those facing loss to share more honestly than perhaps is possible with close family members for whom they feel responsible.

Reflection 1

All praise to the God and Father of our Master, Jesus the Messiah!
Father of mercy!
God of all healing counsel!
He comes alongside us when we go through hard times, and before you know it, he brings us alongside someone else who is going through hard times so that we can be there for that person just as God was there for us.

(2 Corinthians 1: 3-4 *The Message*)

What does this say to you as a church visitor going to see those who have been bereaved?

Reflection 2

I am certain that nothing can separate us from his love: neither death nor life, neither angels nor other heavenly rulers or powers, neither the present nor the future, neither the world above nor the world below – there is nothing in all creation that will ever be able to separate us from the love of God which is ours through Christ Jesus our Lord.

(Romans 8: 38-39 *GNB*)

Paul's affirmation of faith has given many people hope. Are there any Bible verses or hymns/ psalms/ songs that have helped you as you consider death and bereavement?

Is there any way you might be able to share these with a bereaved person?

Reflection 3

No one ever told me that grief felt so like fear. I am not afraid, but the sensation is like being afraid. The same fluttering in the stomach, the same restlessness, the yawning, I keep on swallowing… At other times it feels like being mildly drunk or concussed. There is a sort of invisible blanket between the world and me. I find it hard to take in what anyone says. Or perhaps, hard to want to take it in. It is so uninteresting. Yet I want the others to be about me. I dread the moments when the house is empty. If only they would talk to one another and not to me.

C.S.Lewis

In these early stages of grief, the need for company and conversation is felt. What are some of the helpful things that people have done for you in your times of bereavement? If you have not suffered a close bereavement, what do you think a church visitor might be able to provide to a person who has been bereaved?

Verses which have brought comfort to some:

I have only slipped away into the next room
I am I and you are you: whatever we
were to each other, that we still are.

Call me by my old familiar name,
speak to me in the easy way which you
always used. Put no difference into your
tone, wear no forced air of solemnity or sorrow.

Laugh as we always laughed at the little
jokes we enjoyed together. Play, smile,
think of me, pray for me. Let my name be
forever the same as it always was.
Let it be spoken without an effort,
without the ghost of a shadow on it.

Life means all that it ever meant.
It is the same as it always was; there is
absolutely unbroken continuity.

I am but waiting for you, for an interval,
somewhere very near, just
around the corner
All is well

Canon Henry Scott Holland

A Prayer for those who Mourn
God of hope and giver of all comfort,
we commend to your tender care
(name)
who mourn(s) the loss of
(name)
Give (name) the peace
which is beyond all understanding,
and assure (him/her/them) that neither death nor life
can separate them from your love
in Jesus Christ our Lord
Amen

(*Book of Common Order,* adapted)

Further Reading:

A Grief Observed; C.S. Lewis, Faber and Faber, London 1961 - this is a diary of his feelings kept after his wife died of cancer - a very moving description of grief
All in the End is Harvest: ed Agnes Whittaker, DLT/Cruse, London: 1994 - an anthology of poetry and prose.
A Special Scar; Alison Wertheimer, Routledge, London: 1991 - experiences of people bereaved by suicide.
Bereavement; Helen Alexander, Lion, Oxford: 2002 - Personal stories of a wide range of bereavements from a Christian perspective; very readable. www.lion-publishing.co.uk
Caring for God's People, Author, Scottish Christian Press, Edinburgh: 1997 - A video training pack.
Grief Counselling and Grief Therapy, J William Worden, Routledge, London 1991- Readable theory, with lots of case studies.
Living Through Grief; Harold Bauman, Lion Booklet, Oxford: 1999
Living when a Loved One has Died, Earl Grollman, Souvenir Press, London, 1995
Losing a Child; Elaine Storkey, Lion Booklet, Oxford: 1999
Understanding Bereavement; Mind Publications, London: 2003 - A clearly written booklet from the mental health charity
www.mind.org.uk
Water Bugs and Dragonflies; Doris Stickney, Mowbray, London: 2000 - A booklet explaining death to children.
When Your Child Loses a Loved One; Theresa Huntly, Augsburg Minneapolis; 2001
Children and Bereavement; Wendy Duffy: Church House Publishing: London: 2003 - This sensitive guide, simply written, examines the needs of bereaved children of different ages. It looks at events like September 11 and Soham and their impact on children. A detailed resource list of organisations, suitable books and spiritual resources is included. www.chpublishing.co.uk

Resources and Contacts

Church of Scotland Board of Social Responsibility
Specialist counselling throughout the country, contact
Charis House

47 Milton Road East

Edinburgh EH15 2SR

0131 657 2000

www.churchofscotland.org.uk (see listings under Divisional Structures)

Cruse Bereavement Care

Leaflets, booklets and specialist counselling

Cruse House

126 Sheen Road

Richmond

Surrey TW9 1UR

Tel. 020 8940 4818

www.crusebereavementcare.org.uk

SANDS

The Stillbirth and Neonatal Death Society offers telephone support, information and has groups throughout the country.

28 Portland Place

London W1N 4DE

020 7436 7940

www.uk-sands.org

The Compassionate Friends

An organisation of bereaved parents and their families who offer understanding, support and encouragement to others after a child's death. Information and advice is also given to those who are helping the family.

53 North Road

Bristol BS3 1EN

0117 966 5202

www.tcf.org.uk

The Foundation for the Study of Infant Deaths

Offers a 24-hour helpline to anyone who has experienced the death of a baby.

020 7233 2090

www.sids.org.uk/fsid

Visiting those who are in hospital

"I was lying flat on my back. My visitors would sit where I could not see them and then talk to each other over me as if I wasn't there!"

"These good church folk came to see me and told me that I was working far too hard and that was why I had ended up in hospital. I would need to mend my ways. They never asked me how I was!"

Two first hand accounts, humorously told, by Church of Scotland elders. This was their experience of being visited in hospital by other church folk!

Visiting in hospital can be a daunting prospect, particularly for those unfamiliar with the experience. Michael Quoist says:

I had to go through a ward; I walked on tiptoe hunting for my patient.

My eyes passed quickly and discreetly over the sick,

as one touches a wound delicately to avoid hurting.

I felt uncomfortable.

Like an uninitiated traveller lost in a mysterious temple

Like a pagan in the nave of a church.

Prayers of Life, Michael Quoist

There are many confusing feelings being experienced by the visitor in this passage. The need to be quiet, respectful - the feeling of invading someone's privacy at a time when they are really vulnerable, a fear of getting in the way, the stress of searching for the person to be visited, the guilt at not wanting to be there, the sense of being in a totally alien environment, the physical reaction to experiencing the sounds and smells of being in hospital, the powerlessness, anger and frustration of not being able to heal someone and walk home with them. Do bear in mind that even if you, the visitor are not experiencing this, a family member or other visitor may be feeling this way. Negotiating or overcoming those feelings can be difficult.

The following suggestions might help in this process:

> Do surround everything in prayer, focusing on the person's need rather than on your anxiety. Imagine Jesus being there at the bedside with you bringing his healing and calm.

> Check beforehand with the minister or family that it is appropriate for you to visit and when might be the best time to do so. Sometimes sending a card or a letter might be a better way of expressing pastoral care. Check also what, if anything, you might take with you. Small change for the shop might be more appreciated than another bunch of grapes which the person is not allowed to eat anyway! Prepaid cards and a pen might be more useful than a novel which the person lacks the concentration to read. An audio book or music tape might be very acceptable as long as a personal stereo is available.

> Be on time. Waiting for a visitor can be a stressful experience. If family is there do give them priority. Don't overstay your welcome. If the person looks tired, ask if you should leave. Just because you have had a long journey to the hospital does not mean that a long visit is justified! The story is told of one church visitor who tried very hard to wake up the patient so they could talk to them! Another walked behind the screens to find an intimate procedure in process! Do appreciate that hospital routines can upset your best-planned visits.

In visiting, our main aim is to be alongside the person, not just to cheer them up. Sitting in silence, just holding someone's hand can be a valued visit. Touch is important for most people as is the smile of one who is glad to see them. Listening to what the person has to say comes first. Open questions such as 'How have things been in the last few days?' or 'In what way might we be able to put that right?' can open up meaningful conversations and assure the person that they are the centre of your concern. The topic of their illness should not be avoided but bringing news of friends, family and church can be appreciated as welcome contact with the outside world. Reassuring the person of the prayers of the church family might be in the form of leaving a prayer card. This kind of card can also be useful to leave if you have not managed to speak to the person or if they might quickly forget that you have visited. Some might appreciate the visitor saying a short prayer.

Practically, an offer to visit the shop for them or attending to some laundry might be welcome. Passing on information or thanks to the nursing staff might be useful. Contacting the hospital chaplain might be something the patient would appreciate.

Remember, too, the needs of the family or carers. Talk to them and listen to how they are coping.

Visiting a confused elderly person in care will be very different from visiting a young person in traction. But the general attitude of the visitor needs to be the same, focusing on the person to be visited, listening for their needs and knowing that God is there, in every situation.

> Eileen Shamy, a Methodist minister from New Zealand, recounts a visit to Jim, living in a nursing home at the age of 76, who had not spoken for several months because of the communication problems he was experiencing through Alzheimer's disease. She was discouraged because she felt her visits were doing no good, but on this visit she took along a small bunch of lily of the valley flowers. "Look, look what I have brought you - smell!" Jim did and suddenly he started to tell her about his boyhood garden. The staff were amazed at this sudden breakthrough. Eileen always took flowers with her on subsequent visits.

When visiting someone who is suffering from dementia - either in their own home or in a nursing home - remember that their prime difficulty is communicating with others. Do stand, sit or kneel in front of the person to maintain eye contact. Check that they can see and hear you and that a television in the corner is not providing an added distraction. A smile and appropriate touch can communicate your care. Do give the person your name and where you are from, always speaking slowly and clearly. What may seem an unproductive silence to you may be the time the person needs to gather their thoughts together to speak to you. Asking questions can cause agitation in the person as they struggle to understand and find a reply. As Eileen Shamy discovered, taking something released Jim to speak. Photographs, music, a football scarf might be examples of things that could evoke memories and encourage the person to talk.

> The elderly gentleman in the nursing home marched up and down constantly, The pastoral visitor fell in step with him and discovered that the elderly gentleman was marching with his regiment back in World War I! Imagine his surprise when the visitor found that they had been in the same regiment! A point of contact had been made.

The person with dementia may immediately forget the conversation but nursing staff say that the person has a peace and contentment afterwards which is almost tangible.

If, as part of pastoral caring, a worship service is held in a nursing home where some might be suffering from dementia, it is important to remember the importance of familiar hymns and readings, the symbolism of a simple cross and the bread and wine of communion.

As the disease progresses and the person becomes increasingly frail and withdrawn and all communication seems at an end, pastoral visitors have been surprised to hear an "amen" as they have shared a simple prayer with the person.

It is suggested that one in five people over the age of eighty will develop dementia, but younger people can also be affected through, for example: Huntington's disease, Down's syndrome, Aids or Creutzfeld Jacob Disease.

As a pastoral visitor, communicating with someone suffering from dementia can be difficult but not impossible. Caring for their carers and finding out the kind of support they would welcome from the church is important too.

Simon Wilson writes as a thirty-four year old curate in the Church of England. Nine years previously he was the victim of a hit-and-run driver and has been in and out of hospital many times. He says:

> 'Visiting, befriending and caring are outward signs of our inward faith in the grace and love of God… When we visit and care for someone in hospital we are entering a dark and frightening forest with them, but it is only God who can take them by the hand and show them - and us - the way out.'

Simon Wilson

The sense of powerlessness the visitor feels might be most acute when visiting someone who is terminally ill. Elisabeth Kübler Ross MD, in her book *On Death and Dying* based on her experience of working with terminally ill patients, gives a poignant insight into the world of the dying. She found that many dying people wrestled with similar issues and emotions.

Denial
This quite natural reaction to bad news 'there must be some mistake' may take the form of denying the terminal nature of the illness or of the illness itself. When people are absorbing shock, denial can be a protection. Usually it is temporary and will soon be replaced by partial acceptance.

Anger
Sometimes a visitor might feel that doctors, nurses, family and God are being unfairly attacked. Yet an angry reaction, 'Why me?' is natural when death threatens. It is important to listen, to put yourself in the person's position and try to see where the anger is coming from.

Bargaining
'If I recover, I will go back to church…' A visitor can listen and possibly explore the reality of the promises.

Depression

A deep sense of loss may overtake the person e.g.

- loss of strength and abilities
- loss of job and status
- the impending loss of everyone and everything

Listening to anxieties and offering practical support for the person and their families can help. Sharing Christian experience may be appropriate.

Acceptance

As one dying person said of this stage, "It is the final rest before the long journey." The pain has gone, the struggle is over. Communication at this stage may be more non-verbal than verbal. A silent holding of the hand may bring more comfort and reassurance than words.

Elisabeth Kübler Ross found that all these stages did not appear with everyone and the order varied. Hope, she found, runs through them all.

Treating people as individuals, listening and responding to their needs is so important. Labelling people as 'terminally ill' can depersonalise any visit. Listening to the person and their thoughts, feelings and wishes and not just concentrating on their illness can help the visitor to respond in a natural and caring way.

Reflection Points to be considered on your own or with others

Reflection I

Charles Causley, the Cornish poet wrote a humorous poem entitled:

Ten Types of Hospital Visitor

Verse One

> THE FIRST (visitor) enters wearing the neon armour
> Of virtue.
> Ceaselessly firing all-purpose smiles

At everyone present
She destroys hope
In the breasts of the sick,
Who realise instantly
That they are incapable of surmounting
Her ferocious goodwill.

Such courage she displays
In the face of human disaster!

Fortunately, she does not stay long.
After a speedy trip round the ward
In the manner of a nineteen-thirties destroyer
Showing the flag in the Mediterranean,
She returns home for a week
- With luck, longer -
Scorched by the heat of her own worthiness.

Verse Three
The third skilfully deflates his weakly smiling victim
By telling him
How the lobelias are doing,
How many kittens the cat had,
How the slate came off the scullery roof,
And how no one has visited the patient for a fortnight
Because everybody
Had colds and feared to bring the jumpy germ
Into hospital.

The patient's eyes
Ice over. He is uninterested.
In lobelias, the cat, the slate, the germ.
Flat on his back, drip-fed, his face
The shade of a newly dug-up Pharaoh,
Wearing his skeleton outside his skin,

Yet his wits as bright as a lighted candle,
He is concerned only with the here, the now,
And requires to speak
Of nothing but his present predicament.

Verse Six

The sixth visitor says little,
Breathes reassurance,
Smiles securely.
Carries no black passport of grapes
And visa of chocolate. Has a clutch
Of clean washing.

Unobtrusively stows it
In the locker; searches out more.
Talks quietly to the Sister
Out of sight, out of earshot, of the patient.
Arrives punctually as a tide.
Does not stay the whole hour.

Even when she has gone
The patient seems to sense her there:
An upholding
Presence.

Charles Causley *Collected Poems 1951-1975*

What do these verses say to you about meaningful hospital visiting?

Reflection 2

What anxieties might pastoral visitors have in visiting those who know they are terminally ill? What meaningful role might the visitor fulfil for the dying person or for their relatives?

Reflection 3

A prayer before an operation

O God, you understand my feelings at this moment;
you know my fears and my nervousness;
you know the thoughts that I cannot put into words.

I thank you for all the skill and wisdom of the surgeon,
the anaesthetist and the nursing staff.
Give them your strength during all their work today,
And help me to place myself in their hands.

I now place myself confidently in your loving hands,
Knowing that nothing can separate me from your love in Christ Jesus
Like my Saviour long ago, I say to you,
"Father into your hands I commit myself... May your will be done."

Pastoral card, Christian Publicity Organisation
(see www.cpo-online.org)

In what ways might this prayer be useful?

Reflection 4

Looking at the following verses which ones encourage you as you consider life after death?

a) Psalm 23: 4

   Even if I go through the deepest darkness, I will not be afraid,
   Lord, for you are with me.

b) John 11: 25

   Jesus said to her, "I am the resurrection and the life. Whoever
   believes in me will live, even though he dies; and whoever lives
   and believes in me will never die. Do you believe this?"

c) John 14:1-3

Jesus said, "Believe in God and believe also in me. There are many rooms in my Father's house, and I am going to prepare a place for you. I would not tell you this if it were not so. And after I go and prepare a place for you, I will come back and take you to myself, so that you will be where I am."

d) Romans 8, 38-39

Paul wrote, 'I am certain that nothing can separate us from his love: neither death nor life, neither angels nor other heavenly rulers or powers, neither the present nor the future, neither the world above nor the world below - there is nothing in all creation that will ever be able to separate us from the love of God which is ours through Christ Jesus our Lord.'

e) I Corinthians 15, 20

Paul says, 'But the truth is that Christ has been raised from death, as the guarantee that those who sleep in death will also be raised.'

f) I Thessalonians 4, 13-14

Paul says, "Our brothers, we want you to know the truth about those who have died, so that you will not be sad, as are those who have no hope. We believe that Jesus died and rose again, and so we believe that God will take back with Jesus those who have died believing in him."

g) Revelation 21, 1-4

Then I saw a new heaven and a new earth... I heard a loud voice speaking from the throne, "Now God's home is with mankind! He will live with them and they shall be his people. God himself will be with them, and he will be their God. He will wipe away all tears from their eyes.
There will be no more death, no more crying or pain. The old things have disappeared."

GNB

Reflection 5

A Prayer for the Dying

Merciful Jesus Christ,
we remember that on the cross
you gave your spirit
into the hands of your Father.
By the memory of your death,
help us to live day by day for you,
so that, at the hour of our departing,
we may commend ourselves trustingly
to the same everlasting arms,
and be received into your heavenly kingdom,
to dwell with you for ever;
for your endless mercies' sake
Amen

Book of Common Order

How helpful do you find this prayer?
How might you use it?

Further Resources

Caring for God's People, Scottish Christian Press - Video Pack Units on Visiting the Sick and Visiting the Confused Elderly, Edinburgh: 1997
When I Was in Hospital you Visited Me, Simon Wilson, Grove Books, Cambridge, 2001 - booklet provides thoughtful guidance for hospital visitors.
A Need for Living, Tom Gordon, Wild Goose, Glasgow, 2001 - resource book for those visiting the terminally ill, written by a hospice chaplain.
My Journey into Alzheimer's Disease, Robert Davis, Tyndale House, Wheaton Illinois, 1989
On Death and Dying, Elisabeth Kübler-Ross, Routledge, London, 1989
Understanding Dementia, Mind (National Association for Mental Health) - informative booklet, part of a whole series from:
Mind Publications
15-19 Broadway

London E15 4BQ
Tel Mindinfoline: 0845 766 0163
Web site: www.mind.org.uk
In a Strange Land, Malcolm Goldsmith, 4M Publications, Southwell, Notts., 2004
- practical suggestions for how the local church might be involved with people
with dementia
*A Guide to the Spiritual Dimension of Care for People with Alzheimer's Disease and
Related Dementia*, Eileen Shamy, Jessica Kingsley: London: 2003

Prayer Cards: credit card sized, laminated cards which can be personalised
are available from:
Amos Scripture Care Trust
St George's West Church
58 Shandwick Place
Edinburgh EH2 4RT
Tel. 0131 623 7141
www.amos-sct.org.uk

Pastoral cards with prayers and readings:
CPO
Garcia Estate
Canterbury Road
Worthing
West Sussex BN13 1BW
Tel. 01903 266400 (for samples)
www.cpo-online.org

Scripture Selections
Scripture Gift Mission
3 Eccleston Street
London SW1W 9LZ
Tel. 0207 730 2155
www.sgm.org

Scottish Bible Society
7 Hampton Terrace
Edinburgh EH12 5XU
Tel. 0131 337 9701
www.scottishbiblesociety.org

Suffering

Story

"I prayed so hard that my husband would live. He didn't. God ignored my prayers."

The above words were said by a heart-broken widow who had lost the love of her life. Her pain and disappointment were real. Why does God apparently answer some prayers and not others? Why do people have to suffer? Why is life unfair? These are all questions which might be asked of a pastoral visitor. These are questions which a pastoral visitor might be asking of their own experience or that of others.

There are many books on the subject of pain and suffering. The following piece was written by William Barclay, one time Professor of Divinity and Biblical Criticism at the University of Glasgow, and broadcaster and author:

'I believe that suffering and pain are never the will of God for his children. I was never able to say - in the days when I was a pastor of people - to go into a house where someone was stricken with a serious illness - say cancer- or perhaps a condition that would leave life a living death- and say, "This is the will of God."
I could never go into a family where there had been a death by accident or where a young person had died too soon and say, "This is the will of God."
I cannot conceive that it is the will of God that anyone should be run over by a driver under the influence of drink, or that a young mother should die of leukaemia or that someone in the first flush of youth should have to face the increasing helplessness of a muscular wasting disease. When these things happen, I am quite certain that there is no-one sorrier than God.
Some years ago our twenty one year old daughter and the lad to whom one day she would have been married were both drowned in a yachting accident. God did not stop that accident at sea but he did still the storm in my own heart, so that somehow my wife and I came

through that terrible time on our own two feet.

The day my daughter was lost at sea there was sorrow in the heart of God.

When things like that happen there are just three things to be said:

First - to understand them is impossible

Second - Jesus does not offer solutions to them. What he does offer us is his strength and help somehow to accept what we cannot understand.

Third - the one fatal reaction is the bitter resentment which forever after meets life with a chip on the shoulder and a grudge against God. The one saving reaction is simply to go on living, to go on working, and to find in the presence of Jesus Christ the strength and the courage to meet life with steady eyes, and to know the comfort that God is afflicted by my affliction.'

William Barclay

When attempting to accompany someone who has lost a baby; someone who is encountering a life-threatening condition; is facing financial ruin through no fault of their own; is being battered by one loss after another; there are no easy answers to why these things are happening. The challenge for the pastoral carer is perhaps to continue to walk alongside and not abandon the suffering person because there is no answer; there is nothing to say.

The free will we enjoy can sometimes cause others to suffer. Our desire for low prices in the supermarket might cause hardship and suffering to producers at home or in a developing country. Our environmental pollution might cause flooding and devastation elsewhere. Some illness might well be created by our western lifestyle. Even a just war causes the innocent to suffer. All human explanations as to the nature of suffering are limited.

However, no matter how we understand suffering in the context of a loving God, the fact remains that Jesus knew a level of suffering that is hard to comprehend. In Mark 15: 34 Jesus' words, recorded minutes before his death, "My God, my God, why have you abandoned me?" speak of an unbearable desolation. Christians worship a God who has suffered our pain and is not remote from it. Christians worship a God who offers hope and triumph over death through the love of Jesus.

John Wyatt says:

> 'Suffering is not a question that demands an answer.
> It is not a problem which requires a solution.
> It is a mystery that demands a presence.
> Suffering in another human being is a call to the rest of us to stand in community.'

> *Matters of Life and Death*

Standing in community may not be easy but it is part of the challenge of pastoral care.

Reflection Points to be considered on your own or with others

Reflection 1

Read through the book of Job in the Old Testament, preferably in a modern version like *The Message* by Eugene Peterson. Consider where Job's visitors went wrong. In what ways does this story help us as pastoral carers today?

Reflection 2

As you read Professor Barclay's account above (from *Testament of Faith*) what insight does it give you into suffering?

Reflection 3

What kinds of suffering might make it difficult to stand in community?

Reflection 4

Read Isaiah 53. In what ways does this add to your understanding of suffering?

Reflection 5

An unknown author wrote the following poem:

I Asked God
I asked God for strength
that I might achieve.

I was made weak
to humbly obey.

I asked God for health
that I might do greater things.
I was given infirmity
that I might do better things.

I asked for riches
that I might be happy.
I was given poverty
that I might be wise.

I asked for all things
that I might enjoy life.
I was given life
that I might enjoy all things.

I got nothing I asked for -
but everything I had hoped for.
Almost despite myself
my unspoken prayers were answered.
I am among all people most richly blessed.

In what ways does this poem resonate with your experience of life?

Reflection 6

Story

A young mum was visited by her minister. She was angry and resentful about the way God was treating her. Her minister suggested that she should go up the hill at the back of her house and, when she was quite alone, tell God out loud exactly what she was thinking and feeling. A week later when the minister returned she said, "I did what you said. I shouted at God and told him exactly how I was feeling… I was overwhelmed by an amazing sense of peace. I burst into tears."

Have you personally experienced anything like this?

Compare the psalmist's words as recorded in Psalm 13 *GNB:*

> How much longer will you forget
> me LORD? For ever?
> How much longer will you hide
> yourself from me?
> How long must I endure trouble?
> How long will sorrow fill my heart
> day and night?
> How long will my enemies triumph
> over me?
> Look at me, O LORD my God and answer
> me.
> Restore my strength; don't let me die.
> Don't let my enemies say, "We have
> defeated him."
> Don't let them gloat over my downfall.
> I rely on your constant love;
> I will be glad because you will rescue
> me.
> I will sing to you, O LORD,
> because you have been good to me.
> (Psalm 13 GNB)

In what way might this help you as a pastoral visitor?

Are there any similarities here with the young mother's experiences?
Is there any sense in which reflecting on God's goodness in the past
can encourage those who are undergoing suffering?

Further Reading

The Problem of Pain, C.S. Lewis, HarperCollins, London 2002
Where is God when it Hurts?, Philip Yancey, Zondervan, Michigan, 2001
When Bad Things Happen to Good People, Harold S. Kushner, Pan, London 1981
Matters of Life and Death, John Wyatt, IVP, Leicester, 1998 - Today's healthcare
dilemmas, in the light of Christian faith.

Awareness of Loss Situations

By the rivers of Babylon we sat down;
there we wept when we remembered Zion....
How can we sing a song to the LORD in a foreign land?

(Psalm 137: 1&4 *GNB*)

The Israelite exiles had suffered the loss of their homeland and all that was familiar to them and they wept. Today asylum seekers might similarly grieve for the land of their birth. Although we usually associate grieving with the death of someone, there are many situations where people grieve a loss other than death.

Talking about the loss can be a real help:

After working hard for the same company over many years, George was called into the boss's office one Friday afternoon and told that, because of restructuring, his job was being made redundant. He was shocked and numb as he drove home. How would he break this news to his wife and teenage children? How would they cope financially? What if he was too old to get another good job? Talking things over with the family eased his anxiety somewhat. Talking to other people in the church who had gone through similar experiences helped to raise low self esteem. Knowing that others prayed about the situation gave hope. The bunch of flowers, the offer of financial support and professional help from within the church made God's love tangible. George came through this loss a stronger person and stronger in faith because he experienced good pastoral care.

Having a trusted listener helps the healing process:

Colin was 33 when he and his wife decided to separate. In spite of the happiness the birth of their daughter had brought, their relationship continued to deteriorate until they found it hard to be civil to one another. They worried what effect this was having on their child. When the legal documentation was complete, Colin felt a sense of relief. When he was at work his mind was taken up with his job. It was in the evenings and at

weekends that he experienced the emotional roller-coaster of his
separation. He felt guilty. He experienced the tyranny of the 'what ifs?' He
felt the pain of not being a good father, of not seeing his little girl every
day, of missing the stages of her growing up, of the failure of his marriage.
He had to stay away from church. It was all too painful. What kept him in
touch was his elder and long time friend who popped in to see him and
invited him out; who listened when Colin wanted to talk about his feelings
and didn't take sides; who could talk about the football team they both
supported; who prayed for Colin and encouraged him to continue as a
Youth Club leader.

Being alongside can ease the loss:

Alcoholism had caused Veronica to lose her job, her family and her self
respect. As a reformed alcoholic, she moved to a new area and started to
rebuild her life. She attended the local church and got involved with the
activities. Her pastoral visitor and elder became friends and learned a lot
about alcoholism as Veronica shared her story with them. When
Veronica's first relapse came it took everyone by surprise but a small
group from the church came alongside and supported her as she worked
through this difficult time. Over the next three years, whilst she stayed in
the area, Veronica had a number of relapses but the same group offered
their support to her in practical ways and in prayer.

Identifying the loss can help.

Loss of freedom

Tom and Anna moved up from the South when Tom was promoted in his
company. Anna soon got a job as a sales executive and thoroughly enjoyed
the challenge of her job. They got involved with their local church. Rachel
was born a year later. It was when the pastoral visitor whose responsibility
it was to contact new parents visited their home that she realised there
was a problem. The house was in chaos. Anna looked dishevelled and had
a deadness about her eyes. Rachel was screaming the house down. Tom
was in Geneva on business. The visitor managed to calm the baby, make
Rachel a cup of tea and listen to the difficulties that Anna had
experienced that day.

Anna felt as if she had lost control of her life. An irritable baby who didn't want to sleep and take regular feeds was making Anna deeply unhappy. Her mother and sister were unable to come and help because they lived so far away and Anna felt unable to cope. She was at the end of her tether. The visitor offered to put Anna in contact with other mothers in the church and suggested that she might like to talk over her concerns with the Health Visitor. She promised to return in a week's time. Anna's closing remark was that, at the moment, getting Rachel baptised just seemed too much of an effort!

Loss of a Son

When Jason told his widowed mother that he was gay, it felt as if Diane's world had just fallen apart. She felt guilt at having somehow failed to be a good mother, horror that Jason might have contracted HIV/AIDS, shame at what others would think of her and resentment that she would never enjoy seeing and caring for grandchildren. She found it impossible to talk to Jason about it and hoped that it would all just go away, that she would wake up and find that it had all been a bad dream. It seemed as if she had lost a caring, helpful son and gained a stranger whom she could not understand. As a church-goer, Diane could not reconcile what she believed with her son's revelation about his sexuality. It was a friend who worked alongside Diane at the church charity shop that first realised something was troubling her. Together they approached their minister and she became a mediator between Diane and Jason. A new understanding is starting to grow between Jason and Diane.

Loss of a Home

As Henry looked round the room, he saw the grandfather clock ticking away in the corner keeping as good time as it had when his grandfather had given it to him as a 21st birthday present. There was the enormous leather sofa that he and Jean had picked up at an auction when they were first married. How Louise, their tousled red haired granddaughter, had loved to hide behind it and shout "Come and find me"! As he looked out of the window he could see that glorious red rose bush, whose name he could never remember, that Jean had planted to celebrate their Ruby

Wedding. His daughter was right. The house was too big for one person and the sheltered accommodation awaiting him was compact, easy to manage and only a mile down the road. He could take his precious photograph albums with him. There was room for them.

Loss of a Mother

When Mary developed the first signs of dementia, her daughter Emily determined to care for her at home. At first, she managed to juggle her job at the supermarket with caring for her mother. It became increasingly difficult as her mother would forget to put water in the kettle before boiling it and lost all sense of day and night. She went wandering down the street in her nightie at two in the morning, that time when Emily had forgotten to lock the door before going to bed. Friends at work and professionals advised Emily to allow her mother to go into care to which she eventually, reluctantly agreed. It was then that an enormous sense of guilt hit her. Added to that, she began to feel that her life no longer had any purpose. There was no-one to care for, her mother didn't recognise Emily when she visited and even Emily's occasional visits to church seemed empty and meaningless. Her mother's friends seemed to avoid her. It was a chance conversation at the check-out one day which alerted Emily to a mental health group that met in the church.

Many of us experience a sense of loss at transition points in our lives. The loss may feel like a crisis. The Chinese character for 'Crisis' has two symbols: one means danger, the other, opportunity.

Gordon Oliver, writing in *Bereavement*, (St John's Extension Studies) looks at some life events and the losses and gains which might be associated with them.

Life Event	Loss	Gain
Starting school	mother's attention	nurture and growth
Changing school	peer group/ relationships	new friends/ learning
Leaving home	security	independence
Getting married	independence	growth in partnership
Birth of child	freedom	participation in growth
Children leave	identity as parent	freedom
Retirement	work identity	further freedom
Death of partner	couple identity	who am I now?
Approaching own death	bodily life	dying into...?

To be aware of events which might create a sense of loss for those for whom we care is important for pastoral visitors. Having someone who will listen to hopes and fears can be a great help to those who are experiencing a sense of loss. Sometimes as a story unfolds a pastoral carer may become aware that they are out of their depth. Good pastoral care is knowing how and when to refer the person to someone with more experience or training. Respecting the confidentiality of what you have been told means you have to ask permission to refer. The pastoral co-ordinator or minister would be the natural first step. Calling on professional expertise within the congregation might be an option. Linking with others who have shared a similar loss might help. Being aware of self-help and support groups in the community and how they can be accessed would be a useful resource. Having a regularly updated collection of pamphlets, books and videos available would be helpful.

As Christians we believe in a God who walks alongside us in our sufferings and suffers with us. In some way, being with those who are experiencing loss is about coming alongside them through painful times. The following poem expresses that kind of attitude.

> If you walk in front of me,
> I may not wish to follow.
> And please don't walk behind me
> for I don't want to lead.

But should you walk beside me
yesterday, today and tomorrow
then one day, in your presence
God will come and meet my need.

Anonymous

Reflection Points for you to consider on your own or with others

Reflection 1

Make a list of the losses, other than death, you have encountered in your life
(e.g. divorce, moving home, burglary, illness/ surgery, unemployment)

What helped you to come to terms with each loss?

Have you experienced any gains from these losses?

Reflection 2

Write down any hymns, prayers or bible readings that have helped you in a time
of loss.

Are there any of those that you would feel free to share with
someone suffering a loss?

Reflection 3

The writer of Proverbs says, 'Singing to a person who is depressed is like taking
off his clothes on a cold day or like rubbing salt in a wound.'

(Proverbs 25 v 20 GNB)

How might you be able to share something that has been of help to
you in an *appropriate* way?

Reflection 4

When an elderly lady died in the geriatric ward of a small hospital near Dundee,
Scotland, it was felt that she had nothing left of any value. Later, when the
nurses were going through her meagre possessions, they found this poem. What
does it say to you about loss in the ageing process?

An Old Lady's Poem

What do you see, nurses, what do you see?
What are you thinking when you're looking at me?
A crabby old woman, not very wise,
Uncertain of habit, with faraway eyes?
Who dribbles her food and makes no reply,
When you say in a loud voice, "I do wish you'd try!"
Who seems not to notice the things that you do,
And forever is losing a stocking or shoe.
Who, resisting or not, lets you do as you will,
With bathing and feeding, the long day to fill.
Is that what you're thinking? Is that what you see?
Then open your eyes, nurse; you're not looking at me.

I'll tell you who I am as I sit here so still,
As I do at your bidding, as I eat at your will.
I'm a small child of ten... with a father and mother,
Brothers and sisters, who love one another.
A young girl of sixteen, with wings on her feet,
Dreaming that soon now a lover she'll meet.
A bride soon at twenty - my heart gives a leap,
Remembering the vows that I promised to keep.
At twenty-five now, I have young of my own,
Who need me to guide and a secure happy home.
A woman of thirty, my young now grown fast,
Bound to each other with ties that should last.
At forty, my young sons have grown and are gone,
But my man's beside me to see I don't mourn.
At fifty once more, babies play round my knee,
Again we know children, my loved one and me.
Dark days are upon me, my husband is dead;
I look at the future, I shudder with dread.
For my young are all rearing young of their own,
And I think of the years and the love that I've known.

I'm now an old woman... and nature is cruel;
'Tis jest to make old age look like a fool.
The body, it crumbles, grace and vigour depart,
There is now a stone where I once had a heart.
But inside this old carcass a young girl still dwells,
And now and again my battered heart swells.
I remember the joys, I remember the pain,
And I'm loving and living life over again.
I think of the years ... all too few, gone too fast,
And accept the stark fact that nothing can last.

So open your eyes, nurses, open and see,
Not a crabby old woman; look closer... see ME.

Author Unknown

Resources

Mind Publications - helpful booklets for carers or those affected in non-technical
language on various issues affecting mental health
Understanding series includes Dementia/ Post Natal Depression/ Bereavement/
Caring/ Childhood Distress/ Obsessions and Phobias:
Mind Publications
15-19 Broadway
London
E15 4BQ
Tel: 020 8221 9666
www.mind.org.uk

Alzheimer Scotland 24 hour Helpline: 0808 808 3000
www.alzscot.org
gives details of publications and help available to carers and professionals.

Help the Aged provide advice on e.g. residential care, pensions, bereavement. They also provide information on attendance allowance, community care, sheltered housing, and welfare benefits for carers.
Tel; 0808 800 6565
www.helptheaged.org.uk

Self-Help Groups can be found in the front pages of the Thomson's Local Directory which gives contact details for many organisations.

Church of Scotland Board of Social Responsibility. Operationally, the Board's work is split into five geographical areas which cover Scotland. Each division provides a range of services including those for people with dementia, alcohol/drug dependency, learning disabilities, mental health issues. Additional services include counselling services, supported accommodation, community living, homelessness, older people, and children and family support.
Tel: 0131 657 2000
www.churchofscotland.org.uk

Organising Pastoral Care

All the believers lived in wonderful harmony, holding everything in common. They sold whatever they owned and pooled their resources so that each person's need was met. They followed a daily discipline of worship in the Temple followed by meals at home, every meal a celebration, exuberant and joyful, as they praised God. People in general liked what they saw. Every day their numbers grew as God added those who were saved.

(Acts 2, 44-47 *The Message*)

In the very early days of the church, the believers realised the importance of caring for one another, as the above extract from Acts shows.

The organisation of pastoral care in your congregation will depend on the location, size and makeup of your church and community.

The traditional Church of Scotland model is normally geographical. An elder will be responsible for a number of families in a specific area. Usually the elder will visit each family four times a year and make extra visits as needed - visiting in the good times and bad.

This system has certain advantages. Everyone in the congregation, and in some cases the community, is visited regularly.

Visiting

Advantages:

Helps the flow of communication

Enables elders to be in touch with what people are thinking and feeling

Builds up relationships and a sense of community

Allows needs to be identified

Talents to be recognised

Creates opportunities for faith sharing

Vision to be shared

Disadvantages:

Visiting is not everyone's gift

Elders might not have time to do it properly because of work, family, church or other commitments

In some congregations, a large number of elders are required to cover the districts and the Kirk Session might have difficulty in being an effective leadership group through its size

Members of the church and community might not wish to be visited at home by an elder

Visiting is not perhaps the most effective way or indeed the only way of expressing pastoral care for the whole congregation

Different Models

To respond to local needs, different pastoral care models have emerged. Four of these models are described in general terms here:

1. One church member is responsible for the pastoral care of a number of other members, e.g. members of a house group, the young people of the church, or people in the same street or immediate area. Special needs are referred to the pastoral care team.

2. An elder is given responsibility for a number of pastoral visitors. They visit regularly in a specified geographical area and are accountable to one another and the Kirk Session

3. A group of elders work together as a team and share a specified geographical area. Each elder works to their own strengths: one might

organise transport, another social events, another might visit in a care home and organise the weekly service there. Other people are co-opted to the group as required, to work alongside the elders.

4. A group of pastoral care visitors is selected and trained in specific care areas such as bereavement or visiting the housebound, thus complementing the work done by elders.

In organising pastoral visiting and care, whatever model is used, there are a number of important things that visitors need to know:

Why are they visiting?

Is this a general 'keeping in touch' visit?

Is it about building up the sense of Christian community?

Is it to answer a specific need?

Would visitors be expected to provide practical help?

Would visitors be expected to deliver magazines, flowers, tapes of the services, assist at home communion?

Do those visited know why they are being visited?

Do those visited actually want a visit?

Whom are they visiting?

Does the visitor need to have their own transport?

Has the geographical location of those to be visited been taken into account?

Is there a fixed time for visiting?

Has someone personally introduced the new visitor?

Has the new visitor been briefed on whom they are visiting?

Has a letter of introduction preceded the visitor?

Does the visitor have a visiting/ prayer card of some kind to leave with the person?

How is the visiting to be carried out?

Would the visit be weekly/ monthly/ quarterly?

How many people are to be visited?

Would visitors work alone or in pairs?

Would visitors and visited be matched in some way, i.e. should, for example, a male visit a single woman? Would a young person like to be visited by someone much older?

Do those visited know what to expect of the visit?

To whom do the visitors report and how often?

Are written records to be kept? (Remember the Data Protection Act)

Would visitors be expected to organise social get-togethers for those visited, e.g. a garden party for young families, afternoon tea and a short worship service, with transport provided for those normally housebound?

What support can visitors themselves expect?

Have visitors got a job description?

Do visitors know the time commitment expected?

Will their role be reviewed at regular intervals?

Can visitors step down from the task without feeling guilty?

Is there a regular 'get-together' of visitors to discuss issues that arise?

How often can visitors expect training in what they are doing?

What prayer support is available for visitors and those visited?

Do the congregation and community know about the visitors?

Have they been reminded of it recently through the magazine, web site or by prayers said in church?

Do visitors have clear referral guidelines?

Is there an information pack on local resources?

Is there a supply of cards/ books/ booklets/ videos easily accessible to visitors?

Is some form of dedication service offered to visitors?

Suggestions for support and training

'Get-togethers' for visitors

One get-together might have a visiting speaker, perhaps a local doctor or counsellor, to talk about a specific care area such as bereavement. A training exercise or opportunity for feedback and questions might be included.

Another session might use a training video e.g. *Caring for God's People*: Visiting the Confused Elderly, again with an opportunity for feedback.

Another might focus on a more general topic such as the needs of young families. Another might address a questions such as 'Why does God allow suffering?' with input from the minister or a presentation of research into current thinking. (The writings of CS Lewis might be a good place to start, but there are many authors who have attempted to deal with this most important question).

Suggestion: sample programme for a visitors' get-together
Suggested maximum of 12 people, time requirement 90 minutes, venue somewhere comfortable!

Welcome	by co-ordinator
Introduction	for new members of group
Reading	by a member of the group
Prayer	by a member of the group
Task 1	Invite people to share in threes or fours a good experience of visiting Invite some to share with the whole group Invite comment and feedback Spend some time in silent or shared prayer, thanking God

| Task 2 | Invite people in groups to share a difficult experience they have had. (Remind people of the importance of confidentiality - privacy and trust are essential to visiting).
Invite general sharing in the group and constructive feedback as to how situations and skills might be improved. Have other people faced a similar situation? If so, how did they deal with it? If people feel they need more help, would an experienced visiting speaker address the topic?

Spend time in silent or shared prayer bringing these situations and needs before God. |
|---|---|
| Input | By prior arrangement, have a member of the group share a book/ magazine article/ TV programme/ prayer/ web site/ Bible reading that they have found helpful to them in their visiting role. |
| Conclusion | Arrange the date and venue of the next meeting, even a brief discussion of a possible agenda. (Time to reflect on experience needs to be included in any future meeting). |

Close in prayer

After the meeting, the co-ordinator needs to make sure that any suggestions or questions are dealt with as soon as possible.

This programme could be part of a Kirk Session meeting. Timings of course can be adjusted accordingly.

Presbytery Elder Trainers have a number of workshops suitable for pastoral visitors. They include: The Purpose of the Visit, Listening Skills, Caring for the Lapsed, Caring for the Bereaved, Visiting the Sick, Visiting the Confused Elderly, Private Prayer, Praying with Others and Praying as a Group. These are interactive workshops and involve discussion, sharing of experience, thought-provoking input and informative handouts. Your elders will be able to contact your local Trainer, but in case of difficulty contact the Board of Parish Education on 0131 260 3110 or email sheilah.steven@parished.org.uk

In Conclusion

The fourth attempts to cheer
His aged mother with light jokes
Menacing as shell-splinters.
'They'll soon have you jumping round
Like a gazelle,' he says.
'Playing in the football team.'
Quite undeterred by the sight of kilos
Of plaster, chains, lifting-gear,
A pair of lethally designed crutches,
'You'll be leap-frogging soon,' he says.
'Swimming ten lengths of the baths.'

At these unlikely prophecies
The old lady stares fearfully
At her sick, sick offspring
Thinking he has lost his reason -

Which, alas, seems to be the case.

Charles Causley: *Ten Types of Hospital Visitor*

We started with Jesus' words as recorded in John 13: 34, "Now, I give you a new commandment; love one another. As I have loved you, so you must love one another."

We have looked at how that love might be expressed practically and genuinely as people are visited in their homes or in hospital. We have not referred directly to specific areas such as visiting children, young people and those who do not attend church, but hopefully the general guidelines we've given will assist in these situations, supplemented by the further resources suggested.

The kind of pastoral care encouraged by Jesus is, however much broader than visiting. It is about how we, as a church community, relate to others.

How welcome do people feel as they join us for worship, for a baptism, for a wedding, for a funeral?

How welcome do people feel as they use church premises, as they collect their children, as they play badminton, as they come for a coffee morning?

How welcome do people feel when they experience hard times, when they are divorced, when addiction afflicts them, when their money runs out?

It is a challenge to the whole church, not just elders or pastoral visitors, to respond in the loving spirit of Jesus in any situation we might experience. In all our relationships, in the church, at home, at work and at leisure we need to reach out in love. Only then will the criticism that, "The church is full of hypocrites" be finally proved to be untrue.
As Jesus said, "If you have love for one another, then everyone will know that you are my disciples." (John 13: 35 *GNB*)

A Blessing

May the Lord bless you and take care of you;
May the Lord be kind and gracious to you;
May the Lord look on you with favour and give you peace.
(Numbers 6: 24-26 *GNB*)

Acknowledgments

Scottish Christian Press gratefully acknowledges permission to reproduce material from the following sources:

Testament of Faith by William Barclay, published by Continuum

Matters of Life and Death by John Wyatt, published by IVP

'The Hospital' from *Prayers of Life and Death* by Michel Quoist, published by Macmillan (UK) and Sheed and Ward, an imprint of Rowman & Littlefield Publishers, Inc. (USA & Canada)

'Ten Types of Hospital Visitor' from *Collected Poems* by Charles Causley, published by Macmillan

Bereavement by Gordon Oliver, published by St John's Extension Studies, Nottingham

On Death and Dying by Elisabeth Kübler Ross MD, published by Simon and Shuster

A Grief Observed by C S Lewis, published by Faber and Faber

You can make a difference by Tony Campolo, published by Word Books

The publishers apologise for any omissions and will gladly rectify any errors in future editions.

THE LIFE

FRAN

THE LIFE & TIMES OF

Frank Sinatra

BY
Esme Hawes

SIENA

This is a Siena book
Siena is an imprint of Parragon Book Service Ltd

This edition first published by
Parragon Book Service Ltd in 1996

Parragon Book Service Ltd
Unit 13–17 Avonbridge Trading Estate
Atlantic Road, Avonmouth
Bristol BS11 9QD

Produced by Magpie Books Ltd, London

Illustrations courtesy of: Hulton Deutsch Collection;
London Features International; Mirror Syndication
International; Peter Newark's American Pictures

ISBN 0 75251 591 8

A copy of the British Library Cataloguing in Publication
Data is available from the British Library.

Typeset by Whitelaw & Palmer Ltd, Glasgow

HOBOKEN YEARS

In 1914, Hoboken, New Jersey, was a small city with seventy thousand inhabitants. Once a seaside resort for wealthy New Yorkers, it was now an industrial wasteland, flooded by wave upon wave of refugee immigrants to the New World. First, and therefore highest on the social ladder, the Germans arrived, and then the Irish and, finally, the Italians. Amongst the Italians, the northerners considered themselves vastly superior to those from the south – the Sicilians were deemed the lowest of the low.

One of the northern Italians was a pretty 19-year-old Dolly Garavante. When she started dating a 20-year-old boxer called Anthony Martin (Marty) Sinatra, her parents were horrified. He was tattooed, illiterate, asthmatic, unsuccessful as a boxer – and, worst of all, he was Sicilian. Despite her parent's objections, however, Dolly took Marty to the Jersey City registry office on Valentine's day, 1914, and, without further ado, married him.

The young couple were better off than many of their new neighbours since they could, at least, speak English. Dolly's blonde hair and blue eyes enabled her to pass herself off as an Irishwoman, which she frequently did, calling herself Mrs O'Brien. Marty hung around the pool tables and remained a quiet, background figure in her life. Whenever Irish politicians needed Italian votes, they came to the woman with the rough language and the enormous personality and her loud, raucous laugh could be heard all over town. On 12 December 1915, Dolly gave birth to a $13^{1}/_{2}$ pound boy, who was dragged out with forceps which punctured an eardrum, and tore an ear, and gouged his face and neck. The birth was so traumatic that Dolly was never able to have another child so she became fiercely determined to make the most of this one. She also took up midwifery.

Ambitious for her new son, Dolly defied tradition and picked an Irishman instead of an Italian to be his godfather. Dolly was still too ill after the birth to attend the christening and, when the godfather was asked for the name, Frank Garrick, a newspaper manager, absentmindedly gave the priest his own name rather than the one chosen for the new baby, Anthony Martin like his father. The priest duly christened the new baby 'Francis'. When she was told, Dolly thought the accident was a good omen. The boy remained Francis Albert Sinatra.

On 2 April 1917 President Woodrow Wilson declared war against Germany and made Hoboken a principal embarkation port for US troops. The Germans who had run the town for years were either rounded up and shipped to Ellis Island or fled. The Irish suddenly found themselves in charge and moved into the empty German areas of the city, while the Italians flooded into the former Irish areas, and their votes became even more important. Dolly Sinatra was called to the mayor's office where she was given the job of official interpreter to the local court in return for telling the Italians which way to vote in elections. Despite her new and influential position, her own family was constantly in trouble with the law and her youngest brother, Babe, was sent to jail for ten years for his involvement in a murder during an armed robbery.

Once Dolly had firmly established herself as someone who could be guaranteed to deliver the votes, she began to make demands on the local council. In 1927, although there were no vacancies in the fire department, she saw to it that Marty became a fire officer with an annual salary of $2000. Dolly immediately moved the family to a splendid three-bedroom flat slightly outside Little Italy.

Now 12 years old, Frankie, already self-conscious about his facial scars, had become extremely thin and spindly following a recent appendicectomy. His mother, who firmly believed that money solved all problems, dressed him up in expensive clothes (which only made him feel ridiculous); he was the only child in the neighbourhood to have his own bedroom, and when he and his friends started a baseball team, Dolly bought every boy a flashy outfit, thereby ensuring that her son was made captain.

As the local midwife, one of her more lucrative sidelines was performing abortions. Everyone in the local community relied on Dolly to save their daughters from disgrace, though they then snubbed her socially because of her profession. Dolly soon found herself with a steady business, charging $25–50 for the treatment, and the Sinatra house, which was one of the few in the area with some spare cash, was always the scene of parties and noise.

In 1931 Frank started at High School and dashed his mother's high hopes for his academic career by being expelled for 'general rowdiness' after 47 days. Dolly was furious but had to accept it as he did not want to stay at school. She told him to find himself a job. Frank didn't know how to. Dolly rang up his godfather and asked him to give Frank a job at the newspaper. Nobody in their right mind crossed Dolly Sinatra, and Frank was immediately taken on as a delivery boy.

Dolly, however, had grander ideas. Within a few weeks she heard that one of the sports writers had been killed in a car crash. She immediately told her son to go and get the dead man's job. Frank took his mother's advice literally. The next morning he went into the newspaper office, sat down at the dead man's desk and started sharpening pencils. When the outraged editor learned that Garrick had not given the boy the job he demanded that Frank be dismissed on the spot. Frank was furious, blaming everything on his godfather, but there was little that Frank Garrick could do. Dolly never spoke to Garrick again, and it was 50 years before Frank and his godfather were reconciled. 'My son is like me,' Dolly used to say. 'You cross him and he never forgets.'

By 1932 Dolly was wealthy enough to move again – this time to a four-storey house with dazzling, modern decor. She had a baby grand piano, draped with a Spanish shawl, and a gilded birdbath decorated with golden cherubs holding red plastic roses. She continued to perform abortions in the basement, however. One went badly wrong and Dolly was arrested and put on probation for five years. This did not stop her, however, and neither did subsequent arrests, as she knew her political influence would keep her out of jail. Her Irish neighbours, though, were profoundly shocked and ostracized both her and her son, who felt the hurt deeply.

On Saturday nights Marty would go downtown to drink with the lads and Dolly would go out with her friend, Rose. The two women would hit every political meeting in town, drink beer and sing 'When Irish Eyes are Smiling'. Frank hung around with local musicians and sang at school dances, but to his disappointment the local church wouldn't let him perform on their premises because of his mother's reputation. Frank felt terrible. So did his mother. She bought him a PA system and some sheet music and he found that he could come to an agreement with local bands – he would let them have his arrangements, and they would let him sing with them. His singing was not good – some went as far as to describe it as 'terrible', but Frank was extremely pushy and they couldn't say no.

By 1935 Frank had met a local trio called The Three Flashes and they allowed him to hang out with them because he had a car and they didn't. But they wouldn't let him sing. When the trio were asked to sing in a couple of short films Frank begged them, to let him join the band. They wouldn't. With Frank in tears, Dolly got on the phone. That same afternoon Frank was made lead singer.

The shorts took seven days to film and Frank

was paid $10 a day to wear a top hat and mime a song. They were shown at a one-off screening at Radio City Music Hall, New York, in October 1935 and were surprisingly well received. The owner of Radio City asked the boys if they would like to be in his weekly talent contest and, on the big night, the clapometer registered highest for The Hoboken Four, as they now called themselves They were signed up at $50 a week and included in a nationwide tour with sixteen other variety acts, playing in supermarkets and car parks. There was none of mamma's pasta and Frank became homesick. He wrote to his mother that 'there's no place like Hoboken' and Dolly immediately called *The Jersey Observer* and had this printed in the society page.

'RUSTIC CABIN' YEARS

Frank was the only member of the group to take the tour seriously, which paid dividends – every time he crooned in a solo, women in the audience began to swoon. The other band members grew jealous, and would often tease him and beat him up. By the end of the year Frank couldn't stand it any more and he returned to Hoboken.

Back in Hoboken, Frank sang at Italian weddings, and at social clubs for $2 a night,

Frank Sinatra

and haunted music stations, begging them to give him work. Eventually he auditioned for a small roadside club, the Rustic Cabin, whose shows were broadcast once a week on a live link-up to a New York radio station. Frank failed the audition and went home in tears. Once again Dolly got on the phone.

Frank's new salary was $15 a week and for all his arrogant hogging of the microphone and talk about what a massive star he would soon be, no one thought he could sing. At about this time he started dating a woman called Toni Francke. Dolly was furious. On holiday with his aunt the summer before, Frank had met an Italian girl called Nancy Barbato. Nancy's family lived in Jersey City in a wooden house with a porch, which Dolly considered very respectable. Nancy, she thought, was a highly suitable match for

Frank with his first wife, Nancy

Frank. As well as being well off, Nancy was quiet and devout, and Dolly would still be boss. Now, every time Toni came round, Dolly screamed at her, calling her 'cheap trash' and throwing things at her. Soon Toni became pregnant and although she had a miscarriage, Frank insisted that he'd marry her. Dolly decided that it was about time Frank married Nancy Barbato.

When Toni went down to the Rustic Cabin one day, she found Nancy in the front row, claiming to be Frank's girlfriend. A cat fight ensued. Toni stormed home only to reappear very shortly with two policemen and a warrant for Frank's arrest. He was charged with bringing a single female into disrepute under promise of marriage, and taken to the police cells. Toni found him there a little later, sitting on the floor and sobbing his heart out and she agreed to drop the charges if only Dolly would agree to apologize for destroying their relationship.

Dolly agreed to but never did apologize, and, when Frank got home, she ordered her son to marry Nancy immediately. The wedding was set for 4 February 1939. Frank was wretched and none of his friends were invited. It was a miserable affair. The couple moved into a flat in Jersey City and Nancy got a job as a secretary at $25 a week, the same amount as Frank. Frank rarely appeared in the house and spent most of their money on luxury items for himself.

In June 1939 a trumpeter called Harry James, who had recently left Benny Goodman's band to start his own, heard Frank on the radio and turned up at the Rustic Cabin to have a look.

Frank had evidently improved since the early days because Harry immediately offered Frank a contract at $75 a week. Frank made his first appearance with Harry James and his Music Makers at the Hippodrome in Baltimore within a few weeks, singing popular favourites like 'On a Little Street in Singapore'.

FAME AT LAST

That Christmas, in Chicago, the band had
second billing to the Tommy Dorsey
Orchestra, who were very big at the time.
The lead singer of the Tommy Dorsey
Orchestra casually mentioned to his band
leader that he might leave and Dorsey, a
hugely temperamental man, saw this as an
insult and immediately offered Frank the
singer's job instead. Harry James did not hold
Frank to his contract and as soon as he had
prepared his replacement singer, Frank left to

join the Tommy Dorsey Orchestra.

Within a few months Frank had recorded 'I'll Never Smile Again' which went straight to number one and stayed there for weeks. Tommy began putting Frank's name above everyone else's on the billing, and Buddy Rich, their star drummer, in particular resented him and would alter the tempo while Frank was singing. Once, Frank threw a heavy glass jug at his head; on another occasion Buddy attacked Frank with his cymbals. Both could have been seriously injured – yet some years later Frank was to give Buddy, who was setting up his own band, $40,000. The other band members all found him excessively arrogant, but Tommy recognized his talent, and Frank adored Tommy. When Nancy had a daughter, Little Nancy, on 7 June 1940, he made the bandleader her godfather. In all this time, however, Frank never actually appeared at home and made no pretence about his many affairs, complaining openly about his dull and nagging wife.

In October 1940 the band went to Hollywood to appear in their first feature film as the on-stage band. By the second day Frank had met a blonde starlet called Alora Gooding and, within a week, she had moved into his hotel room. She was just the first of many. In May 1941 Frank, aged 25, was voted top band vocalist in *Billboard* magazine and, by the end of the year, he had displaced Bing Crosby as 'most popular singer'. Frank, now more arrogant than ever, was determined to have a solo recording career under his own name. There was little that Tommy could do to stop him and so, though he was now making

$13,000 a year and everyone in the band thought he was totally bananas, Frank left the band and found himself an agent and a recording contract. The gamble paid off. The agency MCA offered Tommy $60,000 ($25,000 from Sinatra) to buy out Frank's contract, and he was soon making records. But Frank never forgave Dorsey for not letting him off his contract without putting up a fight.

In December 1942 Benny Goodman, the King of Swing, was booked to appear in a show at New York's Paramount Theatre. The main singer was Peggy Lee and the manager decided to add scrawny, young Frank as support. The second the little fellow stepped on stage, the girls went mad. A press agent named George Evans was at that show. The next morning he went to see Frank.

George Evans already represented Duke Ellington, Lena Horne, Dean Martin and others of their calibre, and was determined to make his new client the most sensational singer in the country. The next day, he hired twelve girls at a rate of five dollars each and he rehearsed them furiously. He distributed hundreds of free tickets to local schoolchildren so that the theatre was packed out and then he invited the press in to that evening's show to witness the new phenomenon. They arrived to see scores of hysterical girls moaning, fainting, and throwing themselves onto the stage. It was pandemonium. The next day's papers were full of the story. Although only twelve girls had been hired, thirty had fainted and, that evening, queues began to form around the block. The theatre remained sold out for eight weeks and George Evans started up 250

Sinatra fan clubs around the country, constantly feeding the press stories about the insane devotion of Frank's fans.

George created a whole new biography for his client, making him 26 rather than 28 and elevating him from high school dropout to college graduate. He said that Frank had been a sports reporter on the *Jersey Observer* and that both of Frank's parents were born in America where his mother was a Red Cross nurse. He told Nancy to have her teeth capped and her nose altered by plastic surgery and he took her to buy new clothes. Within a few weeks Frank returned to the Paramount and security men had to be hired to stop the girls from swamping the stage. New York City Education Department threatened to press charges for encouraging truancy in teenage girls.

Frank's entourage now included a large number of burly Italian men, including two bodyguards. Every Friday night Frank took the lads to Madison Square Gardens to watch the boxing; here Frank would see his neighbour, Willie Moretti, the underworld boss of New Jersey, who introduced him to other mobsters. Frank and his followers loved the whole scene and imitated the mannerisms of the low-life crooks, thinking that they were manly and tough.

Soon Frank was offered his first real film role, a starring part in *Higher and Higher*. In August 1943 everyone in his entourage except the Nancys (Big Nancy was pregnant) set off for Hollywood where George had booked him in to the Hollywood Bowl to sing with the Los Angeles Symphony Orchestra. It was the first time a popular singer had ever been offered this accolade and, though classical music lovers were outraged, the place was packed out and it was the largest house of the season. By the end of 1943 Frank was the most popular singer in America and, while psychologists explained this by saying that it was mass hysteria induced by the pressures of war, sociologists claimed that it was related to the aspirations of his mainly lower class fans, who saw Frank as the epitome of the American Dream.

Whatever the reason, Frank was not present when Big Nancy gave birth to their son, Frank Jr, on 10 January 1944. He was in Hollywood filming *Step Lively* and starring in a radio show sponsored by Vimms Vitamins. Frank stayed on in Hollywood for almost three months after the birth and he returned to New Jersey for just a few weeks in March to tell Nancy that he now wanted to live in California where he had bought Mary Astor's estate. Nancy was delighted to get away from Dolly, who was enjoying the reflected glory to the full, and she moved out West, taking her five married sisters with her. The change, however, did nothing to improve her marriage and she saw Frank even less than she had done before.

On 28 September 1944, Frank Sinatra was one of the guests at tea at the White House. President Roosevelt was not popular among Italian–Americans and the invitation secured him the support of Sinatra, who campaigned energetically for him. Frank's fans were delighted but the press were not so sure. To many older Americans, Frank was simply a draft dodger who had become extremely rich at home, while their loved ones were dying abroad. This was an accusation which was to haunt Frank for many years. Though no one questioned Frank's popularity as a singer, all sorts of negative reports began to appear in the press about Frank the man. In 1943 a medical examination had disqualified Frank from military service on account of his punctured eardrum, but in 1945 he was called for another medical; this time he was excused from military service under a clause which exempted all 'outstanding athletes and stage and screen stars' as essential to the nation. Mothers all over the country wrote in to newspapers demanding to know why Frank's crooning was considered more essential than their sons' lives. George Evans knew he had to do something and so, just days after peace was declared, he organized a concert tour of Europe, ostensibly to entertain the troops.

Frank's whole gang flew to Rome where he insisted on their staying at the best hotels and on meeting the Pope who had never heard of him. When Frank was finally introduced to the troops there was a lot of initial ill-feeling as they felt he'd been stealing their wives' hearts while they were stuck abroad. Frank played himself up as a victim – a skinny little runt who couldn't stand up for himself – and immediately endeared himself to the men. Though the press were still suspicious – it was the shortest overseas tour any of the celebrities had made to support the troops – some ground was made up.

Frank returned to the States where he immediately caused offence by criticizing the administration of troop entertainment. To save the situation, George Evans quickly built up Frank's persona of one campaigning against racial injustice, against religious intolerance, racial discrimination. Frank was persuaded to make a ten-minute film called *The House I Live In* (1946) which showed him teaching religious and racial tolerance to a bunch of street urchins. It was a PR triumph and Frank went on to give talks on tolerance, soon receiving the first scroll ever presented by the Bureau of Intercultural Education, which was handed over to him by Eleanor Roosevelt herself.

Next to Eleanor's husband, however, the man whom Frank most admired was Benjamin 'Bugsy' Siegel, the West Coast Mafia boss. Handsome and charming, he described himself as a 'businessman' but everyone knew he had been indicted for a number of offences including murder and extortion. Frank would constantly boast about being Bugsy's friend

The Voice

and talk about how many men Bugsy had killed and how he had disposed of the bodies. Although Frank had, by this time, slept with a number of the world's most beautiful women, including Marlene Dietrich, he was genuinely awestruck by the gangland boss and saw him as often as possible, kowtowing to his every need.

In 1946 Frank moved to MGM on a five year contract at $260,000 a year. By this stage his records sold ten million copies a year and, in his new dressing-room, he pinned up a list of the MGM actresses he most desired. As time went on, he ticked them off one by one. But still, his men came before his women. In January 1947, Joe Fischetti, a sworn mafioso and cousin of Al Capone, came to visit Frank. He invited the singer to go and visit the Mafia bosses at their annual convention in Miami before flying on to Havana where their leader, Lucky Luciano, was living in exile. It was the most exciting thing that had ever happened to Frank. He bought some guns and flew straight to Miami where he put on a free show for 'the boys' and then went on to Havana where he met all the Mafia leaders from across America.

George Evans was worried and announced that Frank was soon to appear in a film (*The Miracle of the Bells*, 1949) as a priest and that he would be donating his entire $100,000 salary to the church. Journalists were highly suspicious. Lee Mortimer, the entertainment editor of the *New York Daily*, was one of the few who dared to express his suspicions in print in a review of the film *It Happened in Brooklyn* (1948). Not long after, Frank 'happened' to encounter Lee Mortimer at a nightclub and, when Lee and his companion got up to leave, Frank and his three stooges followed him out of the club where they pinned him to the ground and slugged him several times. Although Frank claimed that Mortimer had started the incident, MGM attorneys encouraged him to settle the matter and, after some negative press, matters were smoothed over, even if the incident did not do Frank's reputation any good.

Since Frank's only successful film to date had been *Anchors Aweigh* (1945) with Gene Kelly, MGM decided to put him back into a sailor suit. The two new films were *Take Me Out to the Ball Game* (1948) and *On the Town* (1949). Frank, who was now 34, adored Gene Kelly and was very sensitive about his own inferior dancing skills and his receding hairline. He also had to have his large ears taped back for

Anchors Aweigh

every shot and his childhood operation scars covered over with make-up. To add to his humiliations, the costume designer discovered that none of the sailor suits fitted Frank because he had no buttocks. His trousers had to be artificially padded.

Frank and Ava Gardner, 1948

AVA GARDNER YEARS

By 1948 Frank rarely saw his wife, though they did have a second daughter, Christina, born in June of that year. There was no shortage of glamorous women for Frank, but it was 'class' he was after. His greatest hope was to be seen as 'classy' and his greatest aspiration was to capture the heart of the 'classy' star, Ava Gardner. So far, the few times they had met had left Ava unimpressed. Then, one evening they got drunk together and Frank drove her out to the desert, taking his guns along for the ride. They drove through a little desert town, shooting at shop windows, streetlamps, and even hitting a man, though fortunately he received nothing worse than a graze. The pair were immediately arrested and locked up in the local cells. George Evans's partner, Jack Keller, received a telephone call from Frank in the middle of the night, demanding assistance.

Jack arrived within hours and, while Frank and Ava slept in the cells, he sorted the whole matter out. The arresting officers were given $2000 each, $1000 was needed to destroy the hospital records of the injured man and $2000 to repair damaged city property; and $5000 was given to the chief police officer who organized the deal. The shop owners got a $1000 each, and the man who had been injured got $10,000. Ava and Frank were then put on the first plane back home and Jack told Frank in no uncertain terms that he had to stop seeing Ava immediately. Frank was not a man to take orders lightly (or at all). He rang George, demanding that Jack Keller be sacked. Though Frank was still his biggest client, George Evans still had moral scruples and refused to be dictated to by Frank. He, too, advised Frank to stop seeing Ava. After eight years of loyal service, Frank promptly sacked the man who had made him a star.

Ava Gardner was born in 1922 in North Carolina, the daughter of an alcoholic tobacco-cropper. Even as a child, she was stunningly beautiful. At the age of 18 she went to New York to visit her sister who was married to a photographer. He took some pictures of her which ended up in the hands of Louis B Mayer, the head of MGM, who sent for her to come to Hollywood. 'She can't act,' he said, 'she can't talk, but she's a terrific piece of merchandise.' She was signed up for seven years and immediately sent to work with a voice coach since her southern accent was totally impenetrable.

By the time she met Frank Sinatra, she was a different woman. She had already been married twice – first to Mickey Rooney (1942) and then to Artie Shaw (1945), and, in some ways she and Frank were perfectly suited. They were both lean and lithe, both totally uneducated, and both drank like fish. Without George Evans around, there was nobody able to hold Frank back from a tempestuous affair with Ava.

In 1949, however, there were no Sinatra discs

among the best-selling records and people were beginning to think that the dog might have had his day. His films weren't doing too well and his teenie fans had all grown up. Instead of revitalizing his career, Frank squandered all his energies on Ava and, in December 1949, he flaunted all social conventions by taking Ava with him to New York where he wanted her to meet his mother. A few days later, after a short conversation with Nancy in which she refused to agree to a divorce, he walked out on his wife for good.

The publicity was horrendous. Frank was depicted as a total cad and Ava was labelled a home-wrecker. Frank told the papers that his marriage was over a long time before he ever started seeing Ava but nothing could help his negative image. Still loyal to Frank, George

Frank sings, 1950

Evans argued fiercely in his defence with a journalist and then suffered a fatal heart attack. On 27 April 1950 MGM's publicity department issued a statement announcing Sinatra's departure from the studio. It was a dismissal that had been brewing for some time and now because of the number of enemies he had made over the years, no one now offered him a new contract. Ava had left to make a film in Spain and he could not promise her a wedding since Nancy refused to divorce him. Ava got fed up with waiting and began a very public affair with her co-star, a Spanish bullfighter. Back in New York, Frank's voice began to falter and, on the sixth night of his new concert series, he opened his mouth but no sound came out of his throat. He had been struck down with hysterical aphonia and his vocal chords refused to work. His concerts were cancelled and his life was in ruins. Frank flew straight to Spain where the bullfighter had already told the press that he and Ava were madly in love. Frank said it was lie but flew straight back to California. He was besotted with Ava and, for once in his life, he wasn't getting his own way.

Although she would not divorce him, Nancy did hire a lawyer who negotiated a financial agreement with Frank that was most advantageous to her, but crippling to her husband. He was actually obliged to borrow money as he was no longer getting a salary from MGM, his popularity was waning, and he still couldn't sing. He had made so many enemies that none of the sound editors would help him to engineer his voice, and, though he managed to get a booking for his very first television show, his temperamental behaviour made him impossible to work with and the show was cancelled. Unable to find other work, Frank turned to his friends in the Mafia who got him work at a few night clubs.

In 1950 Estes Kefauver, a Democratic senator, became the chairman of a special government committee looking into the workings of organized crime. In his possession were reams of photos of Frank Sinatra with Lucky Luciano, who was now running an international drugs cartel from Cuba. Frank's presence was requested at the hearings. Frank's lawyer, knowing that a public appearance would finish his career completely, only agreed for his client to testify in strictest secrecy. Frank, though he could not deny that he knew these men, said that he knew nothing about their business interests. He escaped being charged, but the case was kept open.

Frank did at least manage to land the lead part in a film, *Meet Danny Wilson* (the screenplay by a friend of his, the storyline closely resembling Sinatra's own rise to the top), which was released (to no acclaim) by Universal in 1951. Frank had to promise the $25,000 fee to Nancy, and the filming was marred by further emotional outbursts from him, for Ava was now refusing to see him until he was divorced. As soon as he could, Frank hurried to Nevada to take advantage of that state's simplified divorce laws, but Nancy filed papers objecting and refused to agree unless he paid her $65,000 immediately. By October Frank was so desperate to see Ava that he conceded to every one of Nancy's demands and, on 31 October 1951, Nancy was granted a divorce in Santa Monica on grounds of Frank's mental cruelty.

The date for Frank and Ava's wedding was set, then called off after a quarrel, and finally took place on 7 November in Philadelphia and, when they got to the registry office, they were surrounded by reporters. As the magistrate pronounced them man and wife, Frank announced to the guests: 'We finally made it. We finally made it,' and Ava ran across the room and threw her arms around her new mother-in-law. Dolly was delighted. 'She's brought my Frankie back to me,' she was quoted as saying. The two women got on famously; they both thought that Frank was the best singer in the world; they were both fiercely committed Democrats and they both swore like troopers. Dolly blessed the marriage and knew that Ava would do her best to kickstart Frank's lagging career.

During his twelve years with Nancy,

however, Frank had always been in control of events. Ava was a very different kettle of fish. She was wild and independent and she was currently earning a lot more than Frank Sinatra. Having to pay Nancy $150,000 a year made him financially dependent on his new wife and Frank, who had no work of his own, spent his time chasing around after her and carrying her bags. His agency fired him and even his record company, Columbia, refused to renew his contract. Ava's career, meanwhile, was soaring sky-high. MGM offered her a new contract at $100,000 a picture; . . . she went to Africa to film *The Snows of Kilimanjaro* for Twentieth Century-Fox. Frank meanwhile was reduced to playing a concert at a small club back in Hoboken where he was pelted with vegetables and booed off the stage.

FROM HERE
TO ETERNITY

It came to Frank's attention that a new film called *From Here to Eternity* was currently being cast by Harry Cohn, the head of Columbia Pictures. Frank read the script and knew that the part of Maggio was the role he'd been destined to play his whole life. He rang Harry Cohn over and over but Harry wouldn't speak to the washed-up star. Before Ava left for Africa to film *Mogambo* for MGM, she went on a secret visit to see Joan Cohn,

Harry's wife, and begged her to intervene on Frank's behalf. Mrs Cohn was stunned. It was a quite extraordinary course of action and she was touched by Ava's devotion to one she saw as a has-been. She said she would try to help.

Fuelled by desperation, Frank managed to arrange a meeting with Cohn. Cohn pointed out that the part was a proper acting part and Frank was not an actor, but Frank begged and made such wild promises that Cohn left him with a 'we'll see'. Frank then sent his agents to see the director Fred Zinnemann (who said much the same thing as Cohn) and himself spoke to the producer of *From Here to Eternity*, and to a few friends . . . Eventually, assaulted on all sides, Cohn agreed that Sinatra might be given a screen test sometime.

The Sinatras soon left for Nairobi, celebrating

their first wedding anniversary on the way. Frank gave Ava a marvellous diamond ring without telling her that he had charged it to her own credit card. 'It was quite an occasion for me,' she said, 'I had been married twice before but never for a whole year.' Just five days later, Frank received a cable saying that he could now do the screen test for *Eternity* and, despite Ava being ill and unhappy, he flew straight back to Hollywood.

Everyone was surprised to see him in the studio so soon after he'd received the telegram. He didn't need the script, he'd already learnt every word of the text by heart and, though he was better than expected, he wasn't, by any means, brilliant. Harry Cohn wanted Eli Wallach to play the part. Eli's screen test was in a different league from Frank's but Eli wanted a lot of money (and had been offered a stage part he was ready to pull out of the film for). Frank was now offering to do the part for nothing. Ava rang Harry from Africa and said that if Frank didn't get the part, he would kill himself and, in the end, Harry didn't know what to do. He chewed his nails and then asked his wife to watch the two tests and see what she thought. Joan agreed that Eli was a better actor but, she said, he looked too healthy. Remembering Ava, she pointed out that Frank was skinny, pathetic and Italian-looking – the right man for the job. Frank got the part.

Back in Africa, Ava had received her credit card bills. She was furious. But Frank was oblivious to the trouble his tempestuous marriage was in. He was working with Montgomery Clift, Burt Lancaster and Deborah Kerr and he was a model of good behaviour. He gave press interviews and he was humble and polite. He rehearsed with Clift constantly and, since neither man could stand to be alone, they drank together all night and Burt Lancaster often had to put them to bed in the early hours of the morning. *From Here to Eternity* was the biggest money-spinner in Columbia's history, all five leading players were nominated for Oscars and, surprisingly, the best reviews came for Frank, who immediately proclaimed his comeback. He was convinced that both his career and his marriage would be salvaged but Ava wasn't so sure.

'When he was down and out, he was so sweet,' she said, 'but now he's back on top again, it's hell. He's become his old arrogant self.' He started drinking with his old Mafia friends and expected Ava to answer to his beck and call. She would not. He, in turn, wouldn't go to the opening of *Mogambo* unless she called him personally. The situation was stalemate and, on 29 October 1953 MGM announced that their marriage was over. Frank was devastated. Alone in New York, Frank half-heartedly, slit his wrists; his agents announced that he was 'physically exhausted'.

Suddenly Frank could sing again and the heartbreak he felt over Ava meant that he now expressed himself with more emotion than he had ever done before. He poured his heart out into ballad after ballad and created a whole new audience of broken-hearted men who all identified with his feelings of loss and betrayal. A non-productive one-year contract with Capitol was renewed and Nelson Riddle became his musical arranger. The combination soon paid off. The partnership lasted eight years and Frank made what are considered to be his best recording during this period including 'Come Fly With Me', 'Young at Heart' and the LP *Songs for Swingin' Lovers*.

Frank brooded over Ava. He called her constantly in Rome and in Madrid and visited her but she wouldn't change her mind. He spent his evenings at nightclubs and playing cards, and got drunk and maudlin. When he took women out he would bore them by talking about his wife and telling them that she was the most beautiful woman on earth. On 25 March 1954 Frank took Little Nancy, now 13, and Frank Jr, 10, to the Oscar ceremony where he received the Best Supporting Actor award for *From Here to Eternity*. It was the biggest night of his life but, after returning the children to their mother, he spent the rest of it alone.

JFK YEARS

At this time Las Vegas was the only place in the US where gambling was legal and Frank bought a share in one of its larger casinos, the Sands Hotel. The management wanted him in so that he would attract punters by performing and, though he frequently spent all of his money at the gambling tables, this was his favourite ever investment. He had a permanent suite in the hotel with a private swimming pool where he regularly held wild parties complete with mandatory orgy

Come Fly with Me

sessions. Frank loved Las Vegas.

In 1954 Sinatra was once again rated most popular male vocalist in a poll, and named Singer of the Year. And during that year and 1955 he made more movies than any other Hollywood star including *Guys and Dolls*, *The Tender Trap*, and *The Pride and the Passion* with Cary Grant and Sophia Loren. By 1956 he was friends with many film folk; in particular, he idolized Humphrey Bogart who was everything Frank aspired to be – educated, sophisticated and respected. Shortly after they became close, however, Bogart was diagnosed as having throat cancer and Frank became a constant visitor to the house and got to know Bogart's wife, Lauren Bacall, particularly well. On 14 January 1957 Bogart died and, for the rest of that year, Frank and Bacall were seen out together constantly. She clearly wanted to marry him and he finally proposed on 11 March 1958 but left the very next day for Miami. That evening Lauren was questioned by a journalist who put the news in the next morning's paper. When she finally got him on the telephone, Frank reproached her bitterly and Lauren did not hear from Frank again for years. According to Ava Gardner he said to her that he had never had any intention of marrying 'that pushy female'.

Frank was gradually being accepted as a grand man of the film world and he received $3 million for a three-year contract with ABC television which was one of the hottest deals ever. Although the ratings were low and the series was dropped, Frank didn't seem to care. All he really wanted to do was be in the movies and in 1958, having made some ten films in the last two years, he was rated the biggest money-making film star of the year. (However, he was disappointed that same year not to win the Grammy award for best male vocal – and horrified when Elvis Presley appeared on the scene.) In September 1959 Frank was master of ceremonies at a Twentieth Century-Fox luncheon in honour of President Khrushchev and his wife, at which 400 of Hollywood's most glamorous people turned up. Frank turned on his full charm and good humour, sitting next to Mrs Khrushchev discussing her grandchildren and his children.

In 1959 Frank's life was transformed by his friendship with Peter Lawford whose brother-in-law, John F. Kennedy, was about to stand for President. The politician was brilliant, rich, handsome and everyone adored him. He, in turn, enjoyed romping around

Hollywood with Sinatra, who introduced him to an endless stream of obliging starlets. Frank was dazzled by JFK and threw himself into the presidential campaign with total dedication, briefly interrupting his political activities for Little Nancy's wedding in September 1960 to teenage-idol singer Tommy Sands. She was his favourite child, upon whom he had lavished the most extravagant gifts, including, for her 17th birthday, the States' first pink Thunderbird.

On Election Day, 8 November 1960, the voting was so close that JFK won by a mere 18,000 votes in a total poll of over 68 million. Frank was beside himself with excitement and was convinced that his Palm Springs house would become the President's retreat on the West Coast. In January 1961 he flew to Washington DC with Peter Lawford to organize the inauguration gala of the new President. It was the most exciting day of Frank's life. He spent $90,000 of his own money having commemorative silver cigarette boxes made up and distributed to every table. For the next three hours the stadium was filled with the glitterati of the entertainment world including Ella Fitzgerald, Laurence Olivier, Bette Davis, Gene Kelly . . . At the end, JKF himself came on stage and thanked everyone involved but particularly Frank Sinatra. Frank was in heaven. He paid to have the President's entire speech reprinted in *Variety* and then had a recording made which he played over and over to his friends.

Returning home to LA was an anti-climax and Frank sat around his pool with a gang of friends, including Marilyn Monroe and

Sammy Davis Jr, and kicked his heels. Though JFK was very grateful to Sinatra, he was never invited to the White House and, anyway, Jackie Kennedy wouldn't let him in. Soon there was a new reason for this. JFK appointed his brother, Bobby, Attorney General and encouraged him to set up a new task force against organized crime. Included in the initial list of top suspects were most of Frank's closest friends. Both JFK and Bobby agreed that, under no circumstances, could the President ever stay at the home of a man who had also played host to known Mafia bosses. Frank couldn't believe it. He'd had a whole presidential wing constructed on his estate specially. He had to blame someone and he chose the unfortunate Peter Lawford as a scapegoat. Peter Lawford was immediately cut out of all Frank's films and his career never recovered.

With President Kennedy, 1961

Frank was filming when he heard the news of JFK's assassination, which devastated him. However, to his deep disappointment, he was not invited to JFK's funeral – the company he was known to keep made him too much of an embarrassment to the Kennedys. Then, just a few weeks later, Frank's son was kidnapped at gunpoint. It was the biggest kidnapping in America for years and gave Sinatra a bad fright. In the event, all went well: Bobby Kennedy immediately had the FBI on the case, Frank paid the ransom and Frank Jr was released; the kidnappers were arrested the next day.

MIA FARROW

In 1964 Frank began filming *Von Ryan's Express*. Towards the end of the shoot a 19-year-old girl with long golden hair appeared on the set. Her name was Mia Farrow. She was a true child of Hollywood, born in 1945 to Maureen O'Sullivan and the director John Farrow. She was in New York playing the heroine in *Peyton Place* a popular television show and she had set her heart on meeting Frank Sinatra. Every day she turned up, in her transparent dress with her wooden beads and hung about the set. After a few weeks she heard Frank talking about going to the desert for the weekend and she ran over straight away and said 'How come you never invite me to come along?' Never one to look a gift nymphet in the mouth, Frank, now almost 50, immediately invited the teenager to join the group and the two became an item.

He called her constantly on the set of *Peyton Place* and the couple told the press that they were in love. She was emaciated-looking and talked about mysticism and extrasensory perception. Frank didn't care. Though she was younger than two of Frank's children, the pair skipped about like young colts and, on 4 July, he gave Mia an engagement ring. After one of his friends told him that he was too old to marry Mia, he arranged the wedding for the very next day and the pair became man and wife on 19 July 1966. No members of Frank's family attended though Dolly later organized a small party at her house. She wasn't impressed. Mia, she said, didn't eat, didn't talk, hadn't ever been in a film. It couldn't last.

Jackie Mason, the comedian, began a routine making fun of Frank's marriage to Mia and he soon began to receive death threats. He didn't change his act and, a few days later, an armed assailant climbed onto his patio and fired three bullets through the window. Some days later a man grabbed him from his car and smashed his face with a metal codger. Other similar incidents occurred whenever anyone tried to criticize Frank. No one pressed charges.

In 1967 Mia was signed up for *Rosemary's Baby*. She also managed to get herself the lead

Frank and Mia

role in a television remake of the film *Johnny Belinda*. Frank couldn't bear the competition and thought that being in films was more important to Mia than her marriage. He did, however, want her to work with him in his next film, *The Detective*. She turned up on the set of *Johnny Belinda* badly bruised and battered, but still wanted to go on. Further dissent in the marriage was highlighted by the war in Vietnam and Mia could not understand Frank's support for the napalm and the agent orange. He got drunk and went to boxing matches. She got stoned, ate yoghurt and meditated. Frank couldn't bear it any more. He told her to stop work immediately on *Rosemary's Baby* in order to start on *The Detective* but Mia just carried on. Frank filed for divorce without even speaking to his wife. Mia was devastated but she agreed to a quick divorce, refusing the generous alimony Frank offered: she didn't want money, she said, she just wanted Frank's continued friendship.

Von Ryan's Express

LATER YEARS

In 1969, Marty Sinatra died, and after much persuasion from Frank, Dolly eventually agreed to move to Palm Springs, where her son built her a fine, large house. That same year saw the release of the album *My Way*, the song of that title having become Frank's signature tune. Also in that year, Mario Puzo's novel, *The Godfather*, was published; it caused Sinatra considerable annoyance as he felt that the character of Johnny Fontane was based on himself – connections with the

Mafia were a sore point. He argued against a subpoena to appear before a New Jersey commission on organized crime, but agreed at last to a secret session in February 1970. There he denied all knowledge of his friends' Mafia connections and was again not charged. It was not the last time this was to happen.

In March 1971, after a year of poor record sales and miserable reviews, Frank announced his retirement. He had made 55 films, over a hundred albums and two thousand recordings. To the astonishment of many people, he suddenly switched his lifetime political allegiance and became involved in the right-wing Republican cause which he had previously detested.

Frank began seeing Barbara, the wife of Zeppo Marx, second youngest of the five

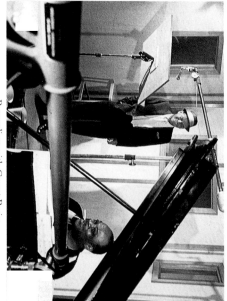

Recording with Count Basie

brothers. After divorcing Zeppo in 1973, Barbara devoted herself to Frank, to whom she was perfectly suited (except in Dolly's eyes) – she was pretty, cheerful, did whatever he wanted and never contradicted him. They finally got married in July 1976, when he was 60 and the bride a respectable 46. Before that, however, Frank started singing again, marking his 1974 comeback with a concert tour of the States, followed by an international tour, Barbara accompanying him everywhere.

In January 1977, Dolly was killed in a plane crash and Frank was beside himself with grief. He turned to the Catholic church for solace and decided that he wanted to remarry his wife before a Catholic priest. Barbara, a Protestant, obligingly converted to his religion. She also began to do serious charity

With daughter Nancy

work and to join all of the most establishment wives' committees. Frank had received several awards for humanitarian acts, having become well known for his spontaneous generosity towards often complete strangers who were in some sort of trouble. The world began to hail the couple as generous sponsors of good causes and, when Ronald Reagan took office in 1981, Frank was once again asked to chair an inaugural gala. Though he hadn't actually been invited to stand on the steps of the White House during the ceremony, he did so anyway and no one dared stop him.

For nearly 20 years Sinatra's gaming licence had been under scrutiny for his violation of Nevada's gaming regulations by allowing certain undesirable characters – i.e. criminals – to frequent his casinos. Eventually, in 1981,

At an awards ceremony with Grace Kelly, Gregory Peck and Barbara

Frank with Nancy Reagan

the Nevada Gaming Board gathered to hear the evidence against Sinatra. Large numbers of key establishment figures and stars testified to his philanthropy and generosity – the state of Nevada had benefited greatly from his actions. Frank denied ever having met most of his best friends. The board renewed Frank's licence for six months: the Nevada Gaming Control Commission, by a vote of four to one, made the renewal indefinite.

Frank no longer made films (apart from the odd cameo role) but he did release a clutch of new records all of which sold incredibly well. He was paid two million dollars for four concerts in Argentina and he also performed at the notorious Sun City resort in Bophuthatswana, South Africa. The United Nations Special Committee against Apartheid placed him top of a list of entertainers who should be blacklisted for supporting apartheid but, by this time, he was untouchable. Nancy Reagan invited him to solo luncheons constantly and she asked him to organize the concert for Queen Elizabeth's visit in 1983 which was generally considered to be a total disaster.

In 1984 Frank was put in charge of fund-raising for the presidential re-election campaign and he did such a fine job that, in 1985, President Reagan awarded him America's highest civilian award, the 'Presidential Medal of Freedom'. In 1986, at the age of 71, he became the oldest person ever to have a hit record in Britain with his recording of the song *New York, New York*, and in 1993 he released a high-tech new album called *Duets*, on which he sang with such stars as Luther Vandross and Chrissie

Frank and Barbara

Hynde. Since he was now somewhat less mobile than in former days, the guest artistes added their vocals to tapes already pre-prepared by Frank. Some singers attended studios while others simply phoned their contributions down digital phone lines. Everyone who was anyone wanted to cut a disc with Frank, even if they weren't to be accorded the honour of actually meeting the star. The record was his biggest success in years and one song in particular, which he recorded with Bono from U2, sold 5 million copies.

Following the popularity of *Duets*, Frank recorded *Duets II* and in 1994 he went to Radio City Music Hall to accept a Grammy award for a lifetime of achievement in the recording industry. Four days later, while singing *My Way* in Richmond, Virginia, he

Frank sings in Oslo

collapsed on stage but by June 1995 he was back on his feet at the grand opening of the new 'Beverly Hills Hotel', alongside Liza Minelli and Sir Anthony Hopkins. The small boy from Hoboken who hung out with hoodlums had made it to the very top where he intended to remain – rich, retired, respected and revered. Dolly would be proud of him.